Digital Photo Suite 2009
User Guide

How to Contact Us

Our main office (UK, Europe):	The Software Centre PO Box 2000, Nottingham, NG11 7GW, UK
Main:	(0115) 914 2000
Registration (UK only):	(0800) 376 1989
Sales (UK only):	(0800) 376 7070
Customer Service/ Technical Support:	http://www.serif.com/support
General Fax:	(0115) 914 2020
North American office (USA, Canada):	The Software Center 13 Columbia Drive, Suite 5, Amherst NH 03031, USA
Main:	(603) 889-8650
Registration:	(800) 794-6876
Sales:	(800) 55-SERIF or 557-3743
Customer Service/ Technical Support:	http://www.serif.com/support
General Fax:	(603) 889-1127

Online

Visit us on the Web at: http://www.serif.com/

International

Please contact your local distributor/dealer. For further details, please contact us at one of our phone numbers above.

Welcome to Digital Photo Suite 2009!

With two products rolled into one, **Digital Photo Suite 2009** offers a truly powerful solution for managing your photo collections.

The exciting **Serif AlbumPlus** and **Serif PanoramaPlus** products, which make up the suite, are fully integrated—you'll get the power of photo editing and photo stitching all from within AlbumPlus! Of course you can use either product independent of each other if you wish!

AlbumPlus X3 AlbumPlus is perfect for creating modern photo albums! The program sports a unique easy-to-use interface, coupled with powerful photo editing, photo searching, and an impressive choice of sharing opportunities.

PanoramaPlus 3 PanoramaPlus intelligently and seamlessly stitches separate photos into fantastic panoramas.

Just go ahead and insert your Digital Photo Suite 2009 DVD to install both programs!

Contents

Contents

Welcome

Welcome

1

Welcome to **AlbumPlus X3**, the powerful and easy-to-use photo manager fully certified for **Windows© Vista**.

AlbumPlus is specifically designed to make it easier and more fun for users to organize and manage their media content within electronic photo albums. Powerful tag searching enables you to easily retrieve photos of those special moments in your life—maybe that first visit to a grandchild, a special wedding for a special person, or your dream holiday.

New features

Sharing

● **Share via Facebook, Flickr and YouTube!** (p. 75)
Upload selected photos and share them via your social networking website, **www.facebook**.com. Alternatively, upload to **www.flickr.com** for worldwide sharing! If your album is packed with slideshows or movies, share them via **YouTube upload**.

● **Flash slideshows**
Wow your friends, family, and colleagues with stunning **Flash slideshows**. Various **gallery styles** offer photo navigation by selection from thumbnail, thumbnail rollovers, photo grid, slide in, or photo stack.

● **Enhanced Menu Designer** (p. 89)
The designer offers **VCD Preview**, **video backgrounds**, and **positioning of menu buttons**. For multi-page VCD menus, each page can adopt its own appearance (e.g., layout, background, etc.). Even more menu background designs are now available.

Photo enhancement

● **Instant Artist Studio** (p. 125)
Turn your photo into a masterpiece with the new **Instant Artist Studio**. Pick from a range of artistic painting styles—don't miss the beautiful **Water Colour**, **Oil**, and **Impressionist** styles!

● **Makeover Studio** (p. 128)
This new and exciting studio delivers professional retouching techniques such as **whitening of teeth** and **eyes**, **smoothing skin**, **blemish removal**, and **reducing under-the-eye shadows**... even get that **instant tan** without the risk of sunburn!

● **Create panoramas**
Make your own panoramas by using Serif **PanoramaPlus**—full integration with AlbumPlus makes for a powerful **photo management - photo stitching** combination.

Ease of Use

● **Tag photos with fun icons** (p. 56)
Preset tag icons can be assigned to photos to aid tag identification, e.g. tag party photos with balloons! Use your own photos to create tag icons.

● **Studio Help assistance**
Instant Artist, Makeover Studio, and QuickFix Studio now have always-at-hand Help panes.

● **Intelligent toolbars**
AlbumPlus is packed with sharing tools. The **Create & Share** toolbar is now context sensitive: tools show only when you need them.

● **Even more powerful multi-tag searching** (p. 63)
Exclude tags from multi-tag searching by **Ctrl**-clicking on any tag's check box.

● **Thumbnail previews**
Hover over any video, audio, or slideshow clip's thumbnail for an instant preview.

● **Import RAW photos, MP3s, and MOVs**
Support for all the latest RAW formats, from all the latest cameras. You can also easily add **MP3 audio** and **Apple QuickTime MOV** files.

File management

● **New Folder View**
Display your album's photos by file location! An Explorer-style pane allows for easy Windows navigation, along with its usual folder and file management capabilities.

● **Watch Folders for newly downloaded photos**
Choose folder locations to bring newly downloaded photo content directly into your album. Ideal for use with digital cameras, mobile phones, photos can be added automatically or you can be prompted.

● **Auto Tagging**
In Folder View, tag photos automatically with their folder names—great if your folders are already categorized by subject matter (e.g., animals, kids, holidays etc.).

● **Full Screen View** (p. 45)
Manage and view photos as big as your screen, while hiding your AlbumPlus user interface. **Rotate**, **zoom**, and **rate** photos from a popup toolbar as you navigate!

● **Sorting your photos** (p. 38)
Photos sorted by date and file location can now be further sorted by photo time, album time, file creation/modification time, and rating.

Photo optimizing

● **Split-screen editing**
For Studio environments, **QuickFix Studio**, **Instant Artist** and **Makeover Studio**, take advantage of before and after views on the same screen—great for side-by-side-comparisons. Drag the dividing line to control how much of the effect you see.

- **Straighten your photos** (p. 123)
  Straighten that otherwise perfect photo with QuickFix Studio's new **Straighten Tool**.

- **Crop to set print sizes** (p. 123)
  Cropping with QuickFix Studio's **Crop Tool**? Pick from a range of preset portrait or landscape photo sizes.

Album management

- **Safeguard your original photos!**
  Protect your digital assets by ensuring that any editing is always performed on a copy of the original—it's easy to revert a photo to any of its former states by using the new Revert Manager.

- **Archive to any media**
  Secure your valuable photo album! Now back up to a different **local/network drive**, **removable device** (e.g., flash drive), or **CD/DVD**.

Existing features

Viewing

- **Viewing your photos**
  Viewing photos is a breeze with resizable thumbnails (double-click for a full screen version). Visual indicators show media type, star rating, comments marker, and the photo's date/time. Hover over Media Type indicator for basic photo information!

- **Calendar-based modes**
  Swap the default **Album View** mode for one of several date-oriented views. **Year View**, **Month View**, and **Date View** modes display thumbnailed photos Year-by-Year, Month-by-Month and chronologically. AlbumPlus can even double up as an electronic diary and events manager so you'll never forget those important dates and events.

Photo editing

- **Edit with QuickFix Studio**
  Correct exposure/colour casts, apply cropping, sharpening, lossless rotation of images and remove red eye. If you want more sophisticated editing, use **Edit in PhotoPlus** for professional level editing facilities.

Photo management

● **Photo addition**
Getting your photo collection into AlbumPlus is straightforward by import from your hard disk or CD/DVD. Alternatively import them directly from your digital camera, scanner, flash card etc. using AlbumPlus's comprehensive device support.

● **Tag management**
Create and assign tags to photos for easy photo retrieval. Display, create, and edit photos' XMP, IPTC, or EXIF tags via Photo Information. Edit a photo's Title, Subject, Authors, Copyright, or Comments. Intelligent tag management preserves the tags of incoming photos.

● **Organize your photos**
Categorize and organize photos to your very own requirements. AlbumPlus's tagging system allows you to create as many categories and sub-categories as you wish without limit, then assign tags to photos by drag-and-drop. Search for photos tagged with single or multiple tags, photo comments, file type/sizes, by import history, or even a particular import session!

● **Photo search**
Powerful searching brings media content to your fingertips easily. Track down your favourite album photos by **Media Type**, **Rating**, **Import History**, **Text** (Metadata including tags), or photo properties from a powerful but easy-to-use search bar. View photos which contain either ALL or ANY matching search criteria via a search results bar. Creative projects can be searched for by Media Type.

Album management

● **Import albums**
Migrate your Serif MediaPlus or Adobe® Photoshop® Elements album to AlbumPlus X3—even rationalize multiple AlbumPlus albums into one. All tags, ratings, and comments are imported.

● **Keep track of your originals**
Fix Links lets you re-establish any broken links between thumbnails and original photos.

- **Backup and restore**
  Perform full or incremental backups to CD/DVD. The album itself is always backed up to ensure none of your information is lost should the very worst happen. Spanning backups across multiple disks is possible for those larger photo collections.

Sharing

- **Calendars**—create month-on-a-page personalized calendars (show diary entries, birthdays, personal/public holidays, and appointments).

- **Postcards**, **photo albums**, and **greetings cards**—each project can adopt an eye-catching range of themes, designs and backgrounds!

- **Photo Disc**—write all or selected album photos to CD/DVD (great for sharing or third-party printing!).

- **Screensavers**—brighten up your computer screen by making a slideshow or flying Screensaver of one or more photos.

- **Slideshow VCD**—write multiple slideshows to VCD with your own customized **Menu Designer** layouts.

- **Slideshow movie**—create standalone MPEG1 or WMV movies!

- **Wallpaper**—set your PC's desktop to be your favourite photo.

- **Send to Email** or **Send to Mobile**—delight your friends and family with a surprise photo (resize options available).

- **Print**—create contact sheets, use paper saving templates for multiple copies or the contemporary print layouts to create compositions ready for display. Preview lets you rearrange photo order, view single and facing pages, auto-rotate images and automatically reflow images as you experiment with the different templates.

Don't forget to register your new copy, using the **Registration Wizard**, also on the **Help** menu. That way, we can keep you informed of new developments and future upgrades!

Installation

If you need help installing Windows, or setting up peripherals, see Windows documentation and online Help.

AlbumPlus System Requirements

Minimum:

● Windows-based PC with DVD drive and mouse

● Microsoft Windows® XP or Vista operating system

● 256 MB RAM

● 529 MB free hard disk space

● XGA (1024x768 resolution, 16-bit colour) display or higher

Additional disk resources and memory are required when editing large and/or complex images.

Recommended:

● 512 MB RAM

● XGA (1024x768 resolution, 24-bit colour) display or higher

Optional:

● Windows-compatible printer

● Scanner and/or digital camera

● CD/DVD writer/rewriter for archiving and creating Slideshow VCDs

● (Windows XP users only) Windows XP (SP2) for writing archives and creating photo discs

● Internet account and connection required for uploading and software auto update

First-time install

To install Serif AlbumPlus X3, simply insert your Program DVD into your DVD/CD drive. If AutoPlay is enabled on the drive, this automatically starts the Setup Wizard. If you are installing AlbumPlus on Microsoft Windows® Vista, you may need to click on **Run autorun.exe** from within the **Autoplay** dialog. If AutoPlay is not enabled (or doesn't start the install automatically), use the Manual install method described below.

1. From the initial screen, you'll be prompted to install **AlbumPlus X3** or **PanoramaPlus 3**. Choose the former option.

2. The Setup Wizard begins with a **Welcome** dialog, click **Next>**.

3. To add customer information, enter your **User Name**, **Organization** (if applicable), and your software **Product Key**.

    For product key information, click ⍰ . Click **Next>**.

4. Please read through the scrollable license agreement, then if you agree to the terms, enable the **I Accept...** button. Click **Next>**.

5. Choose a US or UK language for your install. Click **Next>**.

6. (Optional) Check **Install QuickTime** if you intend to use *.mov files in AlbumPlus. Click **Next>**.

7. Choose Shortcut Options for Start Menu program group, Desktop, and Quick Launch. Click **Next>**.

8. From the **Ready to Install** screen, click **Change...** for a different install location, otherwise click **Install**.

9. The dialog will display a progress bar as the program installs. Installation is completed after you click the **Finish** button.

Your installation is now complete and you can begin using Serif AlbumPlus X3!

Manual install

For manual installation, use My Computer (Windows® XP), or Computer (Windows® Vista), to navigate to the DVD/CD drive in which your AlbumPlus Program DVD is located. Double-click the DVD's icon and then double-click **setup.exe** in the displayed folder. Choose Serif AlbumPlus X3 from the dialog, then follow the on-screen installation instructions as described above.

Repairing or removing AlbumPlus

To repair or remove the installation:

Microsoft Windows® XP:

1. Click the **start** button and select **Control Panel** from the Windows Start menu.

2. Double-click on the **Add/Remove Programs** icon.

3. Locate Serif AlbumPlus X3 in the list of installed programs, then select it.

4. Click the **Change** button to make changes to the install via the Setup Wizard.

Microsoft Windows® Vista:

1. Click the **Start** button and click **Computer**.

2. Click the **Uninstall or change a program** button.

3. Locate Serif AlbumPlus X3 in the list of installed programs, then select it.

4. Click the **Change** button to make changes to the install via the Setup Wizard.

You can also access this via Programs and Features by clicking **Control Panel** from the Windows **Start** menu (or **Settings>Control Panel** from the "Classic" Windows **Start** menu), clicking **Programs** and then clicking **Programs and Features**.

Repairing AlbumPlus

On occasion, it may be necessary to repair your installation of AlbumPlus. This can happen if system files are overwritten by another program or if they are accidentally deleted.

Open the Setup Wizard and select the **Repair** option and click **Next**. Click **Repair**. The repair process will reinstall all files and registry entries, therefore replacing any missing or incorrectly overwritten files. Once the repair has completed, open AlbumPlus.

Removing AlbumPlus

Open the Setup Wizard, select the **Remove** option and click **Next**. Click **Remove** to completely remove AlbumPlus from your computer.

Getting Started

2

Creating a new album

To help you get started quickly on your photo album, AlbumPlus comes equipped with a simple two-step Startup Wizard. This will set up your album project name and its location on your computer and optionally add photos automatically to your album.

If you launch AlbumPlus for the first time or select **File>New...** you will be presented with **Step 1** of the Startup Wizard. The wizard will help you to open an existing album or create a new album.

Step 1

WELCOME TO **ALBUM**PLUS X3

AlbumPlus will organise all of your photos into an album. If this is the first time you've used AlbumPlus, you need to create this album.

○ Open existing album   ● Create new album

Please choose a name for your album.

My Album.sap

Where would you like your album to be saved?

C:\...\...\Documents   Browse...

Next >>   OK   Cancel

To open an AlbumPlus album:

AlbumPlus will automatically reload the album that was last used. However, you can open a different album at any time.

1. Select **File>New**, enable the **Open existing album** option, then click **OK**.
   OR
   Select **Open....** from the File menu.

2. From the dialog, navigate to the AlbumPlus file you want to open.

3. Select the file and click the **Open** button.

To create an AlbumPlus album:

1. Either use the Windows Start button to pop up the Start Menu, select All Programs, and choose the Serif AlbumPlus X3 item (only applies to first run) or select **File>New** in AlbumPlus at any time. The Startup Wizard is displayed.

2. In **Step 1** of the wizard, enable **Create new album**, choose an album name and a location for your proposed album file, e.g. C:\Photos\2005\.

    ● Your album name is based on a standard prefix "My Album" and, if the album name already exists, an additional "[0]", "[1]" ,"[2]" etc. Of course, you can replace the album name with your own choice—as we'll see later. Your album will always be saved in the Serif AlbumPlus (*.sap) format.

    ● You can define your album save location. You can either edit the folder name directly in the text box or use the **Browse...** button to navigate and specify a new location. If using the former method, typing in the new location will automatically create a folder if it does not already exist.

    The directories will be created for you automatically if not already present. Click **Next>>**.

3. In **Step 2** of the wizard, you can choose to search for media files for inclusion in your album immediately.

WELCOME TO **ALBUM**PLUS X3

Would you like AlbumPlus to search your computer and automatically add all of your photos or other files to your album? You can always add photos later using the Add button from the program.

⦿ Yes, please search my computer now.

Search   Pictures   ▾

For   Common Media Files   ▾

◯ No, please skip this step, I'll add photos later.

Back <<   OK   Cancel

To add media straight away, click the "**Yes**" radio button.

- In the **Search** text box, select the drive/device containing your media files from the drop-down menu; choose the **Browse...** button at the bottom of the list to navigate to your folder location.

- In the **For** text box, select the type of file to be added from the drop-down menu, i.e.

Option	File types included
Common Media Files	Includes all Image, Audio, or Video files listed below
All Image Files	bmp, cur, emf, gif (includes animated), ico, img, j2k, jp2, jpeg, jpg, pcx, png, tif, tiff, wmf, spp (Serif PhotoPlus files).
All RAW files	bay, crw, cr2, dc2, dcr, dng, erf, k25, kdc, mos, mrw, nef, orf, pef, pxn, raf, raw, srf, sti, x3f
All Audio Files	mid, midi, mp1, mp2, mp3, mpa, wav, wma
All Video Files	asf, avi, mov, mpeg, mpg, mpv, wm, wmv

OR

To skip adding media until later, check the "**No**" radio button.

4.   Click the **OK** button. The Startup Wizard closes.

When adding files from CD, DVD and digital cameras, you will be presented with additional import dialogs. See Adding Photos to your Album on p. 19 for more information.

> While you are using AlbumPlus, the application operates in auto save mode with background saves occurring regularly. This can be disabled in **File>Preferences**.

Album View

Album View allows you search for photos on the basis of their previously assigned tags, e.g. Holidays and Hobbies. An easy-to-use **Tags** pane lets you click the tag name(s) of interest to display your matching photos in an adjacent main **Photos** pane. Easy retrieval of such categorized photos makes this a key feature of AlbumPlus.

Some simple management tasks can be performed to make the Album View mode operate most effectively. These tasks include:

- Creating and assigning tags (see p. 53)
- Adding comments to photos (see p. 43)
- Changing the photo order (see p. 38)

The powerful search feature allows you to locate photos by checking one or more tags.

Tags pane   Search Results bar

Frequency bar   Photos pane

Search
It's also possible to search for photo comments, ratings, import history, and inherent photo properties by using the **Search** button on the main toolbar.

Adding photos to your album

Get Media
Media is linked to an album in AlbumPlus—the media remains stored in its original location. To add media to your album click **Get Media** on the main toolbar and choose from the following options:

- Add photos from disk

- Add photos from other sources

For a list of supported file formats, see Creating a new album on p. 15.

Adding photos from disk

The procedures for addition of photos from hard disks and from removable media (CDs, DVDs, USB devices, etc.) differ slightly. For the former, the photo addition is straightforward—files are always available. For the latter, an optional step lets you copy photos to your hard drive.

To add photos from a hard disk:

1. Click on the [Get Media] icon on the main toolbar.

2. In the drop-down menu, select **Add photos from disk**.

3. In the displayed dialog box, navigate to the folder containing your photos.

4. (Optional) In the **Files of Type** text box select the type of file to be added from the drop-down menu, i.e.

Option	File types included
Common Media Files	Includes all Image, Audio, or Video files listed below
All Image Files	bmp, cur, emf, gif (includes animated), ico, img, j2k, jp2, jpeg, jpg, pcx, png, tif, tiff, wmf, spp (Serif PhotoPlus files).
All RAW files	bay, crw, cr2, dc2, dcr, dng, erf, k25, kdc, mos, mrw, nef, orf, pef, pxn, raf, raw, srf, sti, x3f
All Audio Files	mid, midi, mp1, mp2, mp3, mpa, wav, wma
All Video Files	asf, avi, mov, mpeg, mpg, mpv, wm, wmv
All Files (*.*)	Use to find the above file types with unusual file extensions.

For adding **specific** files:

5. Select one or more photos. Use **Shift**-click to select adjacent items. **Ctrl**-click to select non-adjacent items.

6. Click the **Open** button to import photos.

Or, for **bulk** addition:

5.   Click the **Get Photos** button at the right of the dialog to import all photos from the selected folder. This will include all photos in sub-folders contained within the selected folder (uncheck the **Sub Directories** button if this is not required).

6.   Click the **Open** button to import photos in bulk.

> If adding tagged photos, you will be prompted to decide how to deal with the tags—ignore, create as new, or map to existing tags (see Importing tags on p. 26).

> If you always organize your photos in the same root folder, e.g. a My Photos folder, why not use the Watch folders function? This way, new content will always be added to your album. (See the Watch folders topic in online Help.)

CD Import

As photos are linked to an album in AlbumPlus, a **CD Import** dialog provides a **Copy item to hard drive** option to copy photos onto the hard disk—this makes the photos available at all times. If this check box remains unchecked, then photos are still added to your album but will remain on your CD/DVD.

To add photos from a CD/DVD:

1. Follow either the standard **Windows** or **bulk** procedure described above.

2. After selecting **Open** or **Get Photos**, the **CD Import** dialog is displayed. Check the **Copy item to hard drive** option.

3. Check the **Maintain directory structure** option to reproduce the folder structure of the CD/DVD on the hard drive.

4. If you want to rename your files, check the **Rename** box and enter a **Name** e.g. Photo, which will make up the file name of each added photo. A number will also be added to each photo as a suffix, i.e. Photo[1].png, Photo[2].png, Photo[3].png, etc

5. Specify a Destination **Folder** for your photos to be copied to. You can either edit the **Folder** name in the text box or use the **Browse...** button to navigate and specify a new location, e.g. C:\Photos\2007\.

6. Click **OK**.

> This copying process may also retrieve archived photos back into your current working environment.

Autoplay

Your computer may have **Autoplay** enabled which means it will be able to detect any new photo content being introduced to your computer from removable devices, e.g. when a CD/DVD is inserted into your CD/DVD reader, or when you plug in a USB flash drive.

A dialog box will automatically be displayed irrespective of whether AlbumPlus is open.

1. Select the option **Import Media into Photo Album**. AlbumPlus is launched automatically if not already loaded.

2. The **Add Photo(s)** dialog is displayed to allow your photos to be added. Note that AlbumPlus has detected the removable disk automatically.

3. Follow the procedure described in "To add photos from a hard disk". A log is made of any additions to your album so you can view photos added on specific dates. See Searching for Photos, By Import History on p. 68.

Import reports

Adding photos is a simple process. However, you may encounter some issues during file addition which may require resolution, for example:

- **Duplicate Photos:** A photo you are trying to add will not be added because it already exists in your album. The duplicate check is based on the file content and not the file name, type or path.

- **Corrupt Photos:** The added photo is corrupt and will not be added to your album. An example would be a WMF file with invalid header or excessive dimensions.

- **Invalid Imports:** The format of the photo means that it cannot legally be decoded by AlbumPlus.

The user is informed of any of the above by the display of an **Import Report** dialog. This will only be displayed if an error occurs. A tree display will indicate error counts for duplicate, corrupt and invalid photos (not shown).

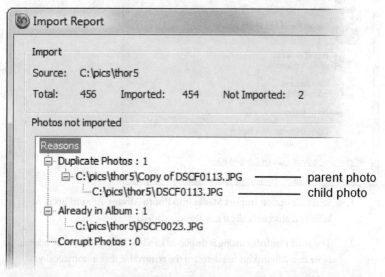

In the above example, for Duplicate Photos, the parent photo listed above the child photo is not added to the album, as the child photo already exists. A photo may be a duplicate even when it has a different file name—photos are always identified by their content.

> Don't let Import Reports stop you from importing from a folder you've imported from before. Only the new files will be added in any case.

Adding files from other sources

Photos may be added into AlbumPlus from a camera, scanner or removable USB flash drive at any time. The process involves the transfer of photos from camera or scanner to a user–defined file folder and then the creation of a thumbnail of each photo.

> If adding photos from a digital camera, this option may not be available if your digital camera drivers/software are not installed correctly.

To add photos from your camera, scanner or removable USB drive:

1. Click on the icon in the main toolbar.

2. From the drop-down menu, select **Add photos from other sources**.

3. From the dialog, select a source for your files (if more than one source exists). The following example imports photos from a Canon IXUS 800 IS digital camera.

Add Photo(s)	
Device	
Source:	Canon DIGITAL IXUS 800 IS
	Removable Disk (O:)
Destination	
Name:	Photo ☑ Rename
Folder:	C:\...\...\Pictures\Serif Browse...
	OK Cancel

4. Enter a **Name**, e.g. Photo, which will make up the file name of each added photo. A number will also be added to each photo as a suffix, i.e. Photo[1].png, Photo[2].png, Photo[3].png, etc. If you want to keep the original filenames, uncheck the Rename option.

5. Specify a **Folder** location to which your photos will be transferred from your camera. Use the **Browse...** button to select a new folder.

6.   Click **OK**.

7.   A manufacturer-specific dialog is displayed to allow your photos to be selected and then added; consult your camera manufacturer's documentation for more information. Note that AlbumPlus has detected the file locations automatically.

8.   Follow either the **specific** or **bulk** procedure described in To add photos from a hard disk on p. 20.

Importing tags

Tagged photos will have typically been assigned tags in AlbumPlus previously or in other album programs such as Adobe PhotoShop Elements. You can also directly tag photos in Microsoft Windows™ Vista.

If tags are detected when adding photos from disk, the **Import Attached Tags** dialog is displayed. From here, you can control how the tags are imported, or choose not to import them at all. By default, AlbumPlus will attempt to map tags that it recognises and create new tags for those that it doesn't.

You can override the default action by choosing an option in the **Action** section:

- **Don't import selected tag**: Images will be imported without the selected tag.

- **Create new tag**: Creates a new, top-level tag. (You can manually reassign tags or modify tag hierarchy at a later date).

- **Map to existing tag**: Links an imported photo tag to an existing tag.

By default, all tags are selected for the chosen action to be performed but you can select specific tags by click select (use **Shift**-click to select adjacent items; **Ctrl**-click to select non-adjacent items).

Mapping your tags

There may be instances when the "incoming" tag name is identical, similar or a synonym of an existing tag. It makes sense therefore to map the tags together, especially if the "incoming" tags have been extensively used in your photos. For example, "holiday" maps to "Holidays", "Vacation" to "Holidays", etc.

To map a tag:

1. Select the "incoming" tag that you want to map.

2. Select the **Map to existing tag** option.

3. From the **New Tag** dialog, choose a tag to map to, then click **OK**.
   If you want to change a mapped tag, click **Choose Tag**. To add a new tag to map to, use the **New Tag** button.

Tag	Action
Events	mapped to "Events" tag
Holidays	mapped to "Vacations" tag
Isle of Man	create new tag
TT	create new tag

> You don't have to create or map all attached tags. Select the ones that you want and select **Don't import selected tag** to ignore the others.

Importing other photo albums

It's simple to combine AlbumPlus albums together, by importing one album into another. It's equally easy to import photo content created in other photo album programs into your currently open AlbumPlus album such as those created in **MediaPlus** or **Adobe PhotoShop Elements** (or **Album**).

Tags, ratings, comments (notes), and any image adjustment information are all preserved during the process, except for any rotation operations carried out on your photos. See Understanding Metadata on p. 57 for more information.

Here's a quick overview of albums you can import.

Album Type	Versions
AlbumPlus	X3 and earlier
MediaPlus	1.0 and 2.0
Adobe Photoshop Album	2.0 and 3.0 Starter Edition
Adobe Photoshop Elements	4.0 and later

AlbumPlus 4.0 and X2 albums can be opened directly in AlbumPlus X3, but the Import Album feature lets you additionally combine albums together from different product versions. Of course, albums created in AlbumPlus X3 can also be combined.

To import albums

1. Load an existing album containing photos or create a new one from scratch.

2. Select **Import Album** from the **File** menu.

3. From the dialog, set the **Files of type** drop-down menu to reflect the type of album to import, i.e.

    ●   an AlbumPlus or AlbumPlus file (*.SAP) for importing
        AlbumPlus and AlbumPlus albums.
        OR

    ●   a MediaPlus file (*.SMA) for MediaPlus albums.
        OR

- an Adobe file (*.PSA) for Photoshop albums.

4. Navigate to the folder of the album to be imported and select the file.

5. Click **Open**. The photos from your imported album will appear in your view.

If any tagged photos are encountered on import, their tags will automatically populate your **Tags** pane. Ratings, comments, and image adjustments will be indicated immediately.

Managing
Photos

3

Selecting thumbnails

Before looking at each of the operations that can be used to manage your photos it's worthwhile familiarizing yourself with the different options available for selecting thumbnails. Selection is the pre-cursor to performing an operation.

The main methods of selection are:

● **Single click:** If you hover over a thumbnail with your mouse, a thin border will appear around your thumbnail. A single click on the thumbnail selects it and the border becomes thicker and light blue in colour.

01/08/2008   10:35:00

● **Drag select:** This is typically used for selecting more than one thumbnail simultaneously. Click next to a thumbnail, hold your mouse button down and drag over your required thumbnails. Release the mouse button when you're happy with the selection.

- Use **Select All** from the **Edit** menu (or **Ctrl**+A)

Alternatively, you can choose a function without selecting any photos at all. AlbumPlus will assume that the requested action (e.g., Slideshow, rotate, print, and email) will be applied to only the current photos in view (excluding photos not visible in the window).

Thumbnail styles

The media files that appear in any AlbumPlus mode will be displayed as thumbnails representing the original media. Thumbnails are very useful as they give you a miniature snapshot of your original photos without having to view every full-size photo in turn. This will help you to move around your albums more efficiently, making photo management so much easier.

To help you remember the media type that your thumbnail represents, when you have Thumbnail Details turned on, an icon will be displayed in the top left corner of your thumbnail.

Here's a quick run down of the main icons you may encounter:

Media

	Image File
	Modified Image File
	Video File (with audio)
	Video File (no audio)
	Audio File
	Unknown media

My Projects

	Slideshow Project
	Slideshow VCD Project
	Calendar Project
	Photo Album Project
	Greetings Card Project
	Postcard Project
	Print Project
	Flash Slideshow Project

If an operation is being performed on a photo, a padlock symbol may appear in the top left corner of the thumbnail (the thumbnail will also be greyed out).

Once the operation is complete the item is unlocked and the padlock icon will disappear.

Thumbnail details 'on':

Thumbnails can be displayed with or without the extra detail—the default thumbnail style is Thumbnail Details on.

Star rating

Media type

Comment marker

Tags

Photo date —— 01/08/2008   10:35:00 —— Photo time

Additional information is displayed alongside the thumbnail. Icons are used to represent the media type, the attached tags, the photo rating and whether or not a comment is attached. The photo creation date and time is also displayed beneath the thumbnail image.

Thumbnail details 'off':

This view is useful if you want to quickly see your album photos and you don't need the additional information.

To view photo information:

● Click [Display] on the main toolbar and select **Photo Information** from
the drop-down list to view file names/locations, file sizes, metadata,
comments, tags, histogram, and EXIF information.

To view/hide thumbnail details:

● Click [Display] and check **Thumbnail Details** to turn details on;
uncheck to turn **Thumbnail Details** off.

Resizing thumbnails

Several methods can be used to set thumbnail sizes to your preferred
dimensions.

● Click on the drag handle at the lower-right corner of the thumbnail
and drag the thumbnail to your chosen new thumbnail size.

● Double-click the thumbnail or press **Ctrl-Tab** to "maximize" it to the
Photos pane. If you double-click again, it will revert back to its original size.

● Choose a pre-defined size: from the menu or via keyboard shortcuts.

● Click [Display] then click **Thumbnail size** and choose a size from
the list.
OR

● Use the keyboard shortcuts: Ctrl-1, -2, and -3 for Small, Medium and
Large respectively.

● With a thumbnail selected, use the magnification slider in the Status Bar to
zoom in or out. Alternatively, click on the Q **Zoom In** and Q **Zoom
Out** icons for magnification in increments. The aspect ratio for each
thumbnail is maintained.

- Click and from the drop-down list, click **Full Screen View**
  OR

  Click 🔲 **Full Screen View** on the Status Bar.

Changing photo order

The thumbnails displayed in AlbumPlus can be sorted in ascending or descending order. This can be carried out on the following sort types:

- Photo Time (time that photo was taken; from Exif)
- Album Time (time photo added to album)
- File Creation Time (time copied to hard disk)
- File Modified Time
- Rating

The file date and times are displayed underneath each thumbnail when **Thumbnail Details** are on.

Photos can be ordered in ascending order which shows the oldest photos first and descending order which shows the newest.

To change photo order:

1. Click on the main toolbar and then click **Sort**.

2. Select a different sort type.

3. (Optional) To reverse the order, select Descending.

Rating your photos

⭐ ⭐ ⭐ ⭐ ⭐ Any photo can be allocated its own star rating. This is really useful when you want to categorize your favourites—assign a rating to your photos and subsequently search for your photos by rating in combination with other tags. See Searching for Photos, by Rating (see p. 66).

Ratings can be from one star to five stars (maximum); five stars would normally be allocated to your most favourite photos.

To rate your photos in the Photo pane:

1. In any mode, select one or more thumbnails.

2. Move your mouse pointer directly above any photo thumbnail. You don't need to select the thumbnail! The ratings setting is displayed as yellow stars as the cursor is moved over the ratings area.

3. Set the required star rating by hovering over the rating that you want to assign.

4. Click the mouse button to assign.

Use your keyboard's numeric keys 1-5 to assign 1 to 5 stars to any selected photos.

To rate your photos in Full Screen View:

1. In any mode, click **Full Screen View**.

2. On the toolbar, click the desired star rating, e.g.

To unassign a star rating:

● Right-click the selected thumbnail(s) and choose **Ratings>Clear** from the flyout menu.

Changing dates and time

When Thumbnail Details are on, the date and time is displayed beneath the thumbnail.

The date and time displayed will always be Photo Time (date and time that photo was taken; from Exif) if available, or File Creation Time (time copied to hard disk) if not.

Any date and time can be altered, however, only the Photo Time is likely to be adjusted, for example:

● You may want a scanned photo to reflect the time the photo was taken rather than when it was scanned.

● When on holiday or business, your digital camera's time zone settings were not adjusted—meaning that the Photo Time is incorrect. Imagine a holiday photo taken at night with a Photo Time set at 13:00:00!

For information on how to search by date see Searching for Photos, By Date (on p. 70).

To change a photo date:

1. Click on the date display in the lower left corner of the thumbnail.

2. Click the down arrow to display a calendar flyout.

3. Click the date that you want to set for the photo. (You can navigate to different months of the year using the left and right arrows.)

4. Click away from the thumbnail to save the change.

To change a photo time:

1. Click the time display in the lower right corner of the thumbnail.

2. Click to highlight the hour, minute or seconds and type in a new value.

3. Click away from the thumbnail to save the change.

   The time is always displayed as the 24-hr clock.

Changing time zones

Suppose you're on holiday and in your excitement you forget to adjust the time settings on your digital camera upon arrival—assuming you've gone somewhere hot, sunny and far away! You've returned home to find that the date and time settings are incorrect. Don't panic—from a single dialog, you can adjust the Photo Time on some or all of your photos to reflect the correct time zone. The dialog is accessible via **Time Zone** on the **Actions** menu, or via right-click. You can change the date and time:

● relative to the currently set Photo Time (see below).
  OR

● by selecting a specific date and time (all selected photos will be set to exactly
  the same time and date).

For example, the above dialog will fix photos with an incorrect date and time
when taken on a holiday in Australia (+11 hours ahead of Greenwich Mean
Time). The adjustment is always made relative to the photo's creation date and
time only.

Setting a specific date and time may be preferred if calculating the difference
between the photo's currently set Photo Time and the required date is too
complicated, or if you know the exact date/time for your photos, e.g. those from
a New Year celebration.

> If the **Specific** date/time adjustment is used, all selected photos will
> have exactly the same time and date as both date and time will be
> applied.
>
> The **Relative** date/time adjustment is better when adjusting
> multiple images in one batch as it preserves the time differences
> between each image.

Instead of the default Photo Time, you can also update times for different time types (i.e., Album Time, File Creation Time, or File Modified Time) via the **Type** drop-down menu.

Adding comments and file information to photos

Why would you add comments? You may already be using tags to identify your photos (see Creating Tags on p. 53) but comments can add more detailed photo-specific notes about the file, for example:.

Type of Comment	Example
Specific photo locations	Sydney
People's names appearing on a photo	Susan with Auntie Jean
Alterations needed	Fix brightness sometime
Funny comments!	Auntie bungee jumping

If a thumbnail has comments associated with it, the comments marker will be displayed in the top-right corner of the thumbnail when Thumbnail Details are on—if there is no comment marker shown this means that no comments have yet been associated.

The addition of more general file information to your photos is also possible. Such information includes Title, Subject, Authors, and Copyright. This information is mostly created as XMP metadata but copyright information is stored as IPTC keyword metadata.

To add comments or file information to a photo:

1. In the **Photos** pane, click to select a photo thumbnail.

2. Click ![Display] and then click **Photo Information.**

3. In the displayed dialog, click ![icon] to show the file information.

4. Click to the right of any Title, Subject, Authors, Copyright, or Comment and type into the displayed white box.

> 💡 It is possible to update the Title, Subject, Authors, Copyright, or Comment information on multiple photos all at once. Simply select all of the images that you want to update before opening the **Photo Information** dialog and make the changes in the usual way.

To view/edit comments/file information in a photo:

● View the **Photo Information** dialog as described above, then if necessary edit any Title, Subject, Authors, Copyright, or Comment accordingly, then click away from the text box.

While it is very useful to be able to read the comments or file information associated with each thumbnail in the **Photos** pane, the real power is in the ability to search by metadata and comments. See Searching for Photos, by Text on p. 63.

Viewing your photos

There are many ways in which you can view your photos:

● Double-click a thumbnail to see it at the maximum size that will fit to the Photo pane (or pressing **Ctrl**-Tab on a selected thumbnail).

● Click 🔲 on the Status Bar to view in full screen mode. You can also edit your photos in this view.

● The ◁ ▷ Navigation buttons on the Status Bar allow you to step through your photos one by one (either forwards or backwards). Try this when your thumbnails are maximised to the **Photos** pane. Alternatively, use the **Page Up** or **Page Down** button.

● Your mouse may have a wheel which will allow you to scroll up/down your thumbnail window or jump to the next or previous photo.

● The photo can be launched in Serif PhotoPlus (see Editing your photos in PhotoPlus on p. 132)—especially if you want to perform some advanced editing of the photo.

● Create & Share. Use for creating photo discs, Slideshows, calendars, photo albums, photo cards, prints, and many more. See Creating and Sharing on p. 73.

> You can also preview your thumbnails without launching your
> associated player—just hover over the thumbnail. To play at full
> resolution, right-click and select Open to launch the file with its
> associated application.

Full Screen View

In Full Screen View, you can manage your photos while viewing them at full
size. In this view, it is possible to rotate, flip, tag and rate your images. You can
even delete them from the album!

To enter Full Screen View:

- Click [⬚] Full Screen View on the status bar.
  OR

- Click [Display] and select Full Screen View from the drop-down list.

Using Full Screen View

The following list is an overview of the available functions from the toolbar:

 See previous photo.

 See next photo.

 Rotate your photo 90° left.

 Rotate your photo 90° right.

 Flip your photo horizontally.

 Flip your photo vertically.

 Opens the **Actions** menu. Here you can perform several
actions, including attaching/detaching tags.

Delete the current photo from AlbumPlus.

Displays one photo at a time in a single page layout.

Displays two photos side by side, in a split screen mode—each with independent control.

Displays two photos, one above the other, in a split screen mode—each with independent control.

Zoom to fit the screen.

Zoom to actual size.

100%   The current level of zoom.

Zoom out.

The zoom level can also be controlled by the slider.

Zoom in.

When selected, the pan and zoom level is synchronized between both photos in split screen view.

Set the star rating on the photo.

Close   Return to your album.

Viewing and editing photos in split screen mode

In the split screen modes, each photo can be viewed and edited independently.

To edit a photo:

1. Click to select the photo you want to change. It will be surrounded by a blue border.

2. Click the relevant toolbar button.

3. The selected photo will be updated.

Synchronized pan and zoom

When the **Pan and Zoom Sync** button is selected, the pan and zoom level of the dual screens are 'locked' together. This means that when you change the zoom level on the selected photo, the unselected photo will also be changed. This is particularly useful for similar images that have had effects applied to them.

Deleting photos

Photos can be removed from your album at any time by a series of methods. It is possible to remove the photo from just your album and from both album and disk at the same time.

To remove a photo from your album:

1. Select your photo(s).

2. From the **Edit** menu, choose **Delete from Album**.

> Remember that you're not deleting your original photo, but the link to the album!

To remove a photo from album and disk simultaneously:

> This method will permanently delete the original file from disc.

1. Select your photo(s).

2. From the **Edit** menu, choose **Delete**.

You'll get a confirmation message asking if you want to delete your photos from disk. If **Yes** is selected, your photo(s) will be sent to your recycle bin (restore from there if you want to revert).

Copying and moving photos

AlbumPlus includes the ability to copy and move photos to new folder locations, without affecting any assigned photo information (tags, ratings, etc.) within the current album.

- Select **Copy to Folder** from the **Actions** menu to copy the selected photo to another folder (using the **Browse to Folder** dialog). The photo's folder location will remain unchanged.

- The **Move to Folder** option moves the photo to the location specified in the Browse to Folder dialog.

Rotating and flipping photos

For more advanced digital cameras, a photo's orientation (portrait/landscape) is detected and stored automatically in the photo's Exif data. This means that AlbumPlus will be able to auto-rotate such photos to their correct orientation as soon as they are imported into your album.

However, for legacy digital content, photo acquisition from more basic cameras, and scanned images, you'll have to manually rotate your photo to its intended orientation; typically by a rotation of 90° clockwise. Of course, you may choose to rotate any photo for artistic reasons at any time.

To rotate a selected photo:

1. Click on the main toolbar.

2. Click 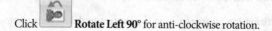 **Rotate Right 90°** for clockwise rotation in 90° intervals.
   OR

   Click **Rotate Left 90°** for anti-clockwise rotation.

To flip a selected photo:

1. Click on the main toolbar.

2. Click **Flip Horizontal** to flip the image horizontally.
   OR

   Click **Flip Vertical** to flip the image vertically.

File management

Most users would normally store their media content on their computer's hard disc, and consequently add photos to albums from there. However, it's also possible to add photos to albums that are stored on removable media such as CDs and DVDs.

This gives an interesting advantage to the user—the ability to manage a CD-based offline photo library without having to copy photos to your hard drive (using up your valuable disk capacity!). However, if you need to perform any **Fix & Enhance** or **Create & Share** operations on photos you need to make them available by inserting the appropriate CD/DVD.

> Fix & Enhance operations will subsequently require the item to be copied to your hard drive before adjustment. This is because AlbumPlus needs to have the original photo at hand to perform writable operations.

> The QuickFix, Instant Artist and Makeover Studios can only perform adjustments on one photo at a time—multiple selections are ignored.

To access photos from CD:

1. Select the photo(s) for use.

2. Choose an operation from the **Fix & Enhance** or **Create & Share** options.

3. If the item is unavailable, you'll be asked if you want to resolve the issues.

4. Click **Yes** (selecting **No** will abort the operation).

5. The **Insert CD(s)** dialog is displayed, which indicates the CD(s), along with unavailable items, which needs to be inserted. Insert the CD.

6. The operation chosen will continue as if the image is stored on your hard drive.

For image adjustments such as QuickFix Studio, Auto Fix, etc., a CD Import dialog ensures that the selected photo has to be copied to a local Folder. (See Adding photos from disk on p. 20).

Using multiple CDs

AlbumPlus lets you fully utilize all CD drives available to you. If selected photos belong to different CDs, AlbumPlus will indicate those CDs as it would for a single CD. For automatic resolution, simply insert each CD into separate drives one by one, or simultaneously.

Consider a two-CD scenario involving unavailable items on a "Fireworks" CD and a "Flowers" CD.

After inserting the "Flowers" CD the flowers photos are made available for use (and removed from the list) but photos on the "Fireworks" CD are still unavailable. Subsequently, inserting the Fireworks CD will automatically resolve this, and remove the dialog.

If you have many photos spread across multiple CDs/DVDs which are all contained within the same album, you may think that a "Catch-22" situation could exist—because there may be insufficient CD drives to make all your photos available. AlbumPlus has a trick up its sleeve to overcome this! Any photos made available are stored temporarily so you can continue to insert then remove the requested CDs until you have cleared all items in the Insert CD dialog. It's a powerful solution that's also very simple.

Setting preferences

You can control global preferences from a **Preferences** dialog, available from the **File** menu. This will enable you to fine-tune some settings to your liking—typically you would set these up at the start of your project or the first time you launch AlbumPlus, changing them infrequently after this point.

Show all warning messages: The **Show All** button is linked to the **All Displayed Photos** dialog, which displays when an action is invoked (e.g., Print) but no items are currently selected. It lets you re-enable the "Don't ask this question again" option in the dialog, if you have previously disabled it. If the **Show All** button is greyed the above option is checked.

Archive: Specifies the interval at which you are prompted to archive your AlbumPlus projects. If archiving is not required, uncheck the box.

Autosave: Sets the interval period between each autosave of your AlbumPlus project file. If autosave is not required, uncheck the box.

Auto Update: Sets the interval period between each prompt to automatically update your program. The auto update enables maintenance releases to be downloaded from Serif. If auto update is not required, uncheck the box.

Audio/Video Preview: Enables or disables the previewing of audio or video thumbnails in your album. A Delay time will set a default number of seconds before a thumbnail preview is seen on hover over. If you have problems playing AVI files on your computer (e.g., codec issues), uncheck the check box.

Creating tags

Before you can use one of the most powerful features of the Album View mode—Photo Searching (see p. 61)—you need to create tag names and then assign the tags your photos. Tags can be associated with any file type or project created in AlbumPlus.

The **Tags** pane can be displayed/hidden by clicking the respective black arrow at the left of your AlbumPlus workspace. It enables you to manage your tags and to control which photos are displayed in the **Photos** pane.

Your new album will be set up with a default tag structure that you can modify at any time.

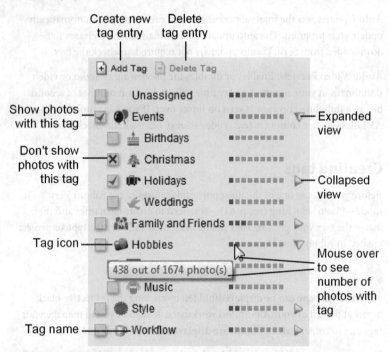

Create new tag entry — Delete tag entry

Show photos with this tag

Don't show photos with this tag

Tag icon

Tag name

Expanded view

Collapsed view

Mouse over to see number of photos with tag

When a previously tagged photo is imported, you can also import the associated tags. This can either create new tags or map to existing tags. See Importing tags on p. 26 for more information.

To navigate the search tags:

In the **Tags** pane, click ▷ to see more tags. To see fewer tags, click ▽.

To create search tags:

1. Click the [+] Add Tag button at the top of the **Tags** pane.

2. The current tag structure is displayed. Click ⊞ to expand or ⊟ to collapse the tag list.

3. Type a new tag name in the **Name:** text box.

4. Click on one of the existing tag names to highlight it. The new tag will be created as a 'child' or sub-level of the selected tag.

5. Click Choose Icon and select an icon from the **Choose Icon** dialog. Click **OK** to apply the tag icon.

6. In the **New Tag** dialog, click **OK**.

> You can also automatically tag photos with their folder name using the Auto tag feature in Folder View.

To delete a tag:

- In the Tags pane, select the tag and click Delete Tag.

  > When you delete a tag from the **Tags** pane, it does not remove that tag from the associated images. Tags must be manually detached from any image that they are assigned to.

To reorganize search tags:

You can reorganize your tags by clicking on the tag name and dragging the tag entry to its new location while holding down the mouse button. Alternatively, to display tags in alphabetic ascending or descending order, right-click on any tag name and check **Ascending** or **Descending**, respectively. Tags on all levels are reordered accordingly. To revert back to non-alphabetic listing, right-click and choose **Custom**.

To rename a tag:

● Click on a tag name in the **Tags** pane to create an insertion point to edit existing text.

To assign a search tag to a thumbnail:

1. Select the thumbnail(s) which are to have the same tag. A blue border will appear around the thumbnail(s).

2. Hold down the mouse button and drag the thumbnail(s) on top of the tag name in the **Tags** pane.
   OR

● Right-click on one or more selected thumbnails, select **Attach Tag**, then select a tag from the root menu or a sub-category.

Your assigned photos can then be searched for. See Searching for photos, By tag on p. 63.

To remove tags from thumbnails:

● Right-click on one or more selected thumbnails, select **Detach Tag**, then select the tag to be removed.

Tag icons

Every tag that is created can be assigned a unique icon. These appear to the left of the photo thumbnail when details are turned on, and give a quick visual reference when viewing your photos in the **Photos** pane.

> Any tag that doesn't have an icon assigned will be represented by 'paper tags' icon. This icon is also used to represent multiple tags when there are too many to fit next to the thumbnail.

To assign a tag icon:

1. In the **Tags** pane, click the empty square (or current icon) next to the tag name.

2. In the **Choose Icon** dialog, choose from one of the following options:

   - **From Gallery** to assign an icon from a set of pre-installed icons.

   - **From File** to create an icon from a file on your hard disc.

   - **From Album** to create an icon from an image within your album.

3. Adjust your icon in the **Preview** pane as necessary. (For more information, see Creating tag icons in online Help.)

4. Click **OK**. Your icon is assigned to the tag.

Understanding metadata

The main strength of modern photo albums comes in their support for various metadata types, all intended to report the photo and file information that will help identify your photo. Three of the most popular metadata formats, EXchangeable Image File (EXIF), International Press Telecommunications Council (IPTC) and the eXtensible Metadata Platform (XMP), are supported within AlbumPlus.

Assigning XMP-based tags, file information, ratings, and comments to a photo means that your album contents can be distinguished from each other by initiating simple searches for such metadata (see p. 57). Read-only EXIF and IPTC metadata can also be viewed (see below) or searched for at any time.

> If you've assigned metadata to a large number of photos and you then attempt to close down AlbumPlus, you may encounter a dialog saying AlbumPlus is currently busy. Select Yes to complete outstanding "tagging" operations (a further progress bar is shown— use the Stop button as a last resort!) or select No to return back to AlbumPlus.

Metadata types

XMP

An editable Adobe XML-based metadata format now superseding IPTC, where data is stored as "keywords" representing the photo's subject matter.

The tags you can assign to your photos from the **Tags** pane are XMP-based—you can create tag names and a tag structure that represents the photo contents of your album (see Creating tags on p. 53). Assigning photos to your tags then becomes a simple drag-and-drop procedure.

You can also view and search XMP metadata and, in particular, modify information such as the photo's descriptive Title, Subject, Authors, Copyright, and Comments.

To display XMP metadata for a selected photo:

1. Click [Display], and then select **Photo Information** from the drop-down list to open the **Photo Information** dialog.

2. Click [icon] at the top of the dialog to show XMP metadata for the selected photo.

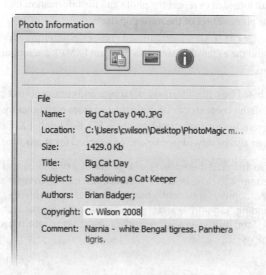

Photo Information	
File	
Name:	Big Cat Day 040.JPG
Location:	C:\Users\cwilson\Desktop\PhotoMagic m...
Size:	1429.0 Kb
Title:	Big Cat Day
Subject:	Shadowing a Cat Keeper
Authors:	Brian Badger;
Copyright:	C. Wilson 2008
Comment:	Narnia - white Bengal tigress. Panthera tigris.

● To modify metadata, click to the right of any Title, Subject, Authors, Copyright, or Comment and type or edit the text in the displayed white box.

EXIF

When using your digital camera, EXIF metadata is associated with your photo irrespective of its file format (RAW, JPG, or otherwise). This information comprises your digital camera's specifications, current photo properties (including size and resolution), and shoot details (time taken, exposure, flash details, white balance, ISO rating, etc.). The information is displayed in a series of fields; the fields listed may vary for photos taken on cameras from different manufacturers. EXIF metadata is read only in AlbumPlus.

EXIF metadata can also be searched for (see p. 63).

To display EXIF data for a selected photo:

1. Click [Display], and then select **Photo Information** from the drop-down list to open the Photo Information dialog.

2. Click [i], and then click the **Exif** tab to view EXIF data arranged into name/value fields.

IPTC

IPTC is an older metadata format (used for news organizations and photo agencies) which contains photo details (including captions, keywords, credits, copyright, photo location and time). IPTC metadata is read only in AlbumPlus.

IPTC metadata can also be searched for (see p. 68).

To display IPTC data for a selected photo:

1. Click [Display], and then select **Photo Information** from the drop-down list to open the **Photo Information** dialog.

2. Click [i], and then click the **Iptc** tab to view IPTC metadata arranged into name/value fields.

Searching for Photos

4

Searching for photos

As befits a powerful photo management program like AlbumPlus, a range of diverse methods exist for photo searching.

- **Tag:** Photos are retrieved by matching tags previously assigned to your photos.

- **Media Type:** This searches for different media formats.

- **Rating:** Searches for personal ratings assigned to your photos.

- **Import History:** Retrieves photos from photo import session logs.

- **Text:** This searches the metadata, comments, tags, file names, paths, and slideshow names associated with your photos.

- **Date:** This searches the dates associated with your photo files.

- **Photo:** Searches for inherent photo properties.

By tag

Searching for photos by tag is exclusively performed from the Tags pane in Album View mode only. A pre-condition is that your photos have been previously assigned one or more user-defined or pre-defined tags. (See Creating Tags on p. 53).

Searches are performed by checking one or more tag entries shown in the Tags pane. Some tags are more general such as Events, Family and Friends>Children, Hobbies, etc. while other more specific user-defined tags can be created within the pane. By checking the tag entry you will display all photos that have been assigned that tag (e.g. all photos tagged with "children").

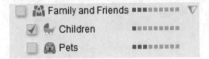

You can perform multi-tag searches by checking multiple tag entries (e.g., all photos tagged with "children" and/or "pets").

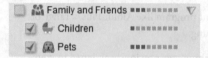

You can also exclude tags from your search (e.g. all photos tagged with "children" but not the ones that also include the "pets" tag). To exclude a tag, **ctrl**-click to select it.

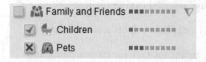

To search by tag:

1.   In **Album View Mode**, ensure the Tags pane is shown.

2.   If necessary, expand the tag list by clicking the ▷ arrows to see the tag you want to search for.

3.   Click to select the box next to a tag name to include that tag. It will display a green check mark ✔.
      OR

      Ctrl-click to select the box next to a tag name to exclude that tag. It will display a red cross ✖.

4.   Your photos will be displayed in the adjacent workspace.

   To start your search afresh, click the Show All Media button to clear all current search tags.

AlbumPlus does a great job in searching for photos with single tags assigned but more powerful multi-tag searching is possible. The **Match All Tags** or **Match Any Tags** options shown after a multi-tag search (see example below) indicates the search results for photos which have to contain all checked tags or photos which can contain any of the checked tags individually. By default, the latter option is used.

Using the "Family and Friends" example above, Match All Tags results will only show photos tagged with both "Children" **AND** "Pets" tags. By contrast, Match Any Tag results will show all photos tagged with the "Children" tag **OR** all photos with the "Pets" tag.

Using the frequency bar

From any AlbumPlus view, it's often useful to be able to see a quick breakdown of the number of photos assigned particular tags. The **frequency bar** on the **Tags** pane is designed with this is mind, and provides a visual indication, both as a bar and pop-up box, of the extent to which photos are tagged with a particular tag in relation to all photos in the current album.

The blue markers on the bar indicate the number of tagged photos vs. all photos in your album. This visual indication is not exact, but gives you a quick snapshot, e.g. in this example, the album has approximately a quarter of its photos currently tagged as "Unassigned".

A pop-up box, can also be displayed by hovering over any frequency bar, and can be used for a more exact analysis, e.g. in the example, 572 photos have the "Family and Friends" tag assigned to them out a total of 1674 photos in your album.

Unassigned status

You may have noticed an **Unassigned** tag at the top of the tag list. Selecting this tag will let you view photos that do not have tags currently assigned. This can be used to separate your "processed" photos from "unprocessed" photos—newly imported photos will often have no tags assigned. As you process your photos you can keep checking their unassigned status by using this method.

By media type

It is possible to restrict searches to specific media types such as Photos, Audio, Video, AlbumPlus projects, or any combination thereof. Projects relate to jobs such as slideshows, prints, etc. which have been saved for future use, all settings having been stored for immediate recall (see Create and Share on p. 75).

To search by media type:

1. Click the [Search] button on the main toolbar.

2. From the displayed search options, click on one or more appropriate media type icons in the **Media Type** box. Matching types are shown in the AlbumPlus workspace.

By rating

The rating level for any photo can be searched for directly from the **Search - Rating** box or from a dialog. The box is used to set the rating level for the search, and the dialog to show items matching at least, at most or exactly to the number of stars set; you can equally just limit the search to unrated items.

Stars have to be assigned to photos in advance, as described in Rating Your Photos on p. 38.

To search for photo ratings:

1. Click the [Search] button on the main toolbar.

2. From the displayed search options, click on a star in the **Rating** box to set the rating level.

3. (Optional) By default, you'll search on "at least" the number of stars set. Click the accompanying ▶ button to alter this to be "at most", "exactly", or "unrated" from a **Filter by Rating** dialog. You can also set the star rating by clicking on a star shown in the dialog.

4. Click the **OK** button.

By import history

Searching by import history lets you display specific photo import sessions used to previously build up your current photo album. From the **Search** feature, the set of thumbnails shown in the **Import History** box represents either the last set of photos imported (by default) or a previous session that you specifically want to search on.

You may want to use this feature to display photos recently added so that you can make image adjustments, or assign ratings and comments to them.

To search by import history:

1. Click the button on the main toolbar.

2. From the displayed search options, check the **Import History** search input box to view just the last set of photos imported.

3. Alternatively, to retrieve a previous import session, click the accompanying ▶ button and select an import session from the displayed dialog, e.g.

Time	Source	Images	Thumbnails
27 August 2008 16:48:51	C:\...\...\Pictures\thor	13/13	
27 August 2008 16:17:06	C:\...\...\Pictures\climbing	25/27	
27 August 2008 14:17:08	C:\...\...\Pictures\surfing	29/30	
26 August 2008 15:25:26	Premium Image Collection 4	61/61	

The display shows sessions from the most recent to the oldest, with the import **Time**, the **Source** folder from which the photos were imported, an **Images** import count (3/4 means 3 photos were successfully imported out of 4—one of the photos may have been a duplicate), and **Thumbnails** representing each imported photo.

4. Highlight an entry in the list (as shown above) to view that session only. Remember multiple log entries can be grouped or selected one-by-one via **Shift**-click or **Ctrl**-click, respectively.

5. Click the **OK** button.

The **Clear** button deselects any highlighted log entries. This means that filtering will not take place when the **OK** button is selected.

If thumbnails have been deleted or have had their "added to album" date modified then there may be a discrepancy between the number or date of the photos displayed in the log information and those shown in the AlbumPlus workspace.

By text

A text search can be performed on added photo comments (XMP), metadata (XMP, IPTC, EXIF), tags, folder paths, file names, and/or slideshow VCD names. For comments, tags, and general file information, you have to add these to your photos in advance (see Adding Comments to Photos on p. 43).

To search for word(s) or phrase(s):

1. Click the [Search] button on the main toolbar.

2. From the displayed search options, type a word or phrase into the **Text** search input box. Only photo comments are searched for by default.

3. Press the **Enter** key to perform the search. Any photos which match are displayed in the **Photos** pane.

To search for specific metadata (file information, IPTC or EXIF), tags, path names, file names, and/or slideshow names:

4. Click the accompanying button to check the option(s) you wish to search on.

5. (Optional) Check the **Case sensitive** box to limit the search to match uppercase/lowercase characters exactly.

6. For multiple words and phrases, check either **Search for all words** or **Search for any words**. For the former, **all** words/phrases must be present; for the latter, **any** of the words/phrases can be present.

7. Click the **OK** button.

By photo properties

The file properties for any photo can be searched on by using a **Filter by Properties** dialog. The minimum and/or maximum levels for width (pixels), height (pixels), bit depth, resolution (DPI) and file size (KB) can be set independently. The specified range will include the actual value proposed for minimum or maximum, as well as the values above or below.

To search for properties:

1. Click the [Search] button on the main toolbar.

2. From the displayed search options, click the button on the right-most **More** box, and choose the **Filter by Properties** tab from the dialog.

3. Click on a check box (minimum or maximum, or both) next to the property you want to search on.

4. Set a value. Use the up/down arrows or type over to change the current value next to the check box.

5. Click the **OK** button. Any photos which match the search criteria are displayed.

For example:

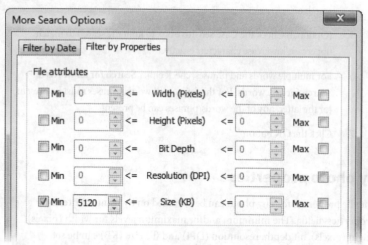

This will show you all photos in your album in excess of 5 megabytes. This will enable you to keep track of your high resolution digital photos (e.g., those in RAW format).

By date

The **Search** feature lets you search for dates when photos were taken, files created or files modified most recently or over a specified time period. In addition, searches can be made on dates on which photos were added to your photo album.

To search by date:

1. Click the [Search] button on the main toolbar.

2. From the displayed search options, click the button on the right-most **More** box, and choose the **Filter by Date** tab from the dialog.

3. Select the check box next to the type of date search you want to use (combinations can be made), i.e.

    ● Photo: Photo Time (time that photo was taken; from EXIF)

    ● Album: Album Time (time photo added to album)

    ● Creation: File Creation Time (time copied to hard disk)

    ● Modified: File modification Time

4. Click the **OK** button.

Creating
and Sharing

5

Create & Share

AlbumPlus is made so much more special by its exciting **Create & Share** features—designed for users who want to take their photo collections beyond the basic store and retrieve functions of most photo mManagement products and into the realms of creative design. You'll get plenty of help in the form of pre-defined layouts, designs, and backgrounds along the way!

 A host of different creative options are available, all accessible from the main toolbar's **Create & Share** button. The toolbar is context sensitive—you'll only see the options available to the type of files you have selected. Here's a quick summary of each option.

 Print photos easily, then store printer settings, layout styles, and the order of photos to a Print Project.*

 Write a selection of photos directly to CD/DVD.

 Create a slideshow of your favourite photos, with supporting transitions.*

 View the slideshow in full screen mode.

 Write multiple slideshows to VCD—all playable from a VCD menu which you can design yourself.*

 Save previously saved slideshow projects to MPG or WMV movie format.

 Create an eye-catching Flash slideshow of your favourite photos, using the stylish transitions and animations.*

View your Flash slideshow in full screen mode.

 Publish your Flash slideshow to a web output folder that can be integrated into your website.

 Send scaled-down photos to an Internet-enabled device (mobile phone, PDA, etc.).

 Send photos to families, friends, and colleagues via email.

 Leaving your PC for a while? Set up either a slideshow or animated screensaver to show off your best photos!

 Pick any single photos to be your PC's background—actual size, tiled, or stretched.

 Create seamless panoramas of several linked images in Serif PanoramaPlus (if installed).

 Adopt calendars made up of selected photos, with different Themes, Designs, and Backgrounds.*

 Create electronic photo albums of your selected photos, using various Themes, Designs, and Backgrounds.*

 Make your own greetings cards with a personal touch.*

 Print simple themed postcards and send them in the post.*

 Upload your favourite albums and images to your Facebook profile.

Upload your favourite photos to flickr, complete with assigned tags and comments.

Upload slideshows and movies straight to your YouTube account.

* These creative options let you save as a project for later playback/ editing.

Sharing photos by printing

Of all the creative avenues open to you in AlbumPlus, you'll most likely visit the Print option most frequently—simply print your favourite photos to your home colour printer at a fixed size, as part of a contact sheet, or by using a layout template.

To print a photo:

1. Select one or more thumbnails. Use **Shift**-click or **Ctrl**-click to select adjacent or non-adjacent items, respectively.

2. Click [Create & Share] and then click [ ] **Print**.

3. From the **General** tab pick your printer, no. of copies and no. of pages to print. A preview window (not shown) lets you check intended output before print.

Printers are selected from the drop-down list; if necessary, click the **Properties** button to set up the printer for the correct page size, orientation, etc.

In the **Finish** section of the dialog, choose whether to **Send to printer** directly, just **Create print project**, or both.

4. Click the **Layout** tab and select your preferred layout style (fixed photo sizes, as contact sheets, or using more complex templates).

5. Click the Items tab to view the item order before printing (rearranging item order is also possible by dragging photo items to the Print Preview window).

6. Click the **OK** button to send the photo(s) to the printer.

Using Print Preview

The Print Preview window is always available to you in the **Print Photos** dialog. This lets you see how your photos will be printed in any layout style.

Page 6 of 7

The following icons let you navigate around the Print Preview window:

 Jumps to previous page

 Jumps to next page

 Displays one page at a time

 Displays two pages at a time

 Zooms out

 Zooms in

 Resets photo order and selection back to that shown in the Items window

When zoomed in, you can use your mouse wheel to scroll the preview window.

If you're using a Landscape Layout template and your Print Preview looks incorrectly aligned, try manually changing the page orientation to Landscape in Printer Properties (**General** tab).

Setting a layout style

When the **Layout** tab is selected in the **Print** dialog, pre-defined layout sizes and styles can be selected with the **Fixed size**, **Contact Sheet** and **Template** options. These enable you to create fixed size prints, use a contact sheet or use print templates (for passport photos, etc.).

- **Fixed size**—decide upon a fixed size by choosing one thumbnail size from several different size options in the dialog.

- **Contact sheet**—lists thumbnails of your photos into any combination of columns and rows.

- **Template**—your photo selection can be arranged onto built-in print templates offering a wide choice of creative layouts in different print sizes and orientations.

For a detailed look at each, see Setting a layout style in the Sharing by printing topic in AlbumPlus online Help.

Using the Items Window

When the **Items** tab is selected in the **Print** dialog, you can reorder your photos for printing by dragging and dropping any photo(s) into a pre-defined position in the print preview window. Semi-transparent placeholders and an "add" cursor will indicate the location to which your photo will be dropped.

Resize the Preview window with the drag handle located in the lower right corner of the dialog.

Creating photo discs

One of the simplest methods to share your photos is to write them to CD/DVD. The ability to create your own disk gives you several advantages over other sharing methods, i.e.

- Send your photo disc to family, friends, colleagues, or drop off at your local print shop.

- Share with users whose ability to connect to the Internet is not known.

- Share a large number of photos without having to upload or email cumbersome attachments.

You can write to your CD drive using CD-R or CD-RW media. For DVD drives, use CD-R, CD-RW, DVD-R, and DVD-RW media.

> If you're looking to backup your photos, remember to use the purposely designed Archive feature in AlbumPlus.

To create a photo disc:

1. Insert your chosen medium into your CD/DVD drive.

2. Select one or more thumbnails. Use **Shift**-click or **Ctrl**-click to select adjacent or non-adjacent items, respectively.
    OR

    Select nothing to write all photos to disc (you'll be asked if you want to do this).

3. Click 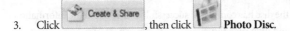, then click **Photo Disc**.

4. From the displayed **Write To Disc** dialog, select the DVD/CD **Drive** to which you want to write your files. The write speed will be selected automatically. Select **Eject disc on write completion** to automatically eject the disc when completed.

5. Click the **Disc info...** button for more options.

6. Give a **Disc label** name to identify the photo disc that is to be created.

7. If you want to create a single-session disc, deselect the **Allow files to be added later** option.

8. Click to select whether to append or overwrite files (re-writable media only).

9. Click **Next**.

10. The dialog will change to show the progress of the write operation, and will provide details such as current task, time remaining, and write progress.

11. When the disc has completed successfully, click **OK** in the information dialog and then click **Finish**.

> All photos on the photo disc are placed in a folder labelled AlbumPlus + date of creation (for example 'AlbumPlus 24 September 2008').

For writing to multiple discs, when you run out of space on your currently loaded disc then a message ("**Please insert another writable disc...**") will be displayed. The write process continues after disc insertion.

Creating slideshows

All or selected photos can be loaded into a step-by-step Slideshow wizard that creates a ready-to-go slideshow that can be played back at any time. You can control the photo order and appearance of your slideshow—add transitions as well as audio accompaniment.

To create your slideshow:

1. Select one or more thumbnails. Use **Shift**-click or **Ctrl**-click to select adjacent or non-adjacent items, respectively.

2. Click [Create & Share] and then click [ ] **Slideshow**.

3. In the first dialog (Items window):

    ● Drag and drop one or more photos to rearrange photo order.

    ● Click [**Add Photos**] to add more photos to your slideshow.

    ● Click [**View Slideshow**] to jump straight to your slideshow.

    ○ You can also use your mouse wheel to scroll the window.

4. In the second dialog (slideshow settings):

    ● Give your slideshow a unique **Name** that you'll remember in the future, e.g. Holiday2007.

    ● If required, check **Stretch to fit** to resize your photos to the screen dimensions.

5. To apply an inter-slide transition:

   ● Choose a transition **Type** from the drop-down menu that will produce a visual effect between each photo.

   ● Set the **Duration** between each photo (this does not include any time allocated to the transition duration).

6. To add a soundtrack:

   ● For accompanying sound tracks, check **Play slide audio**.

   ● For your favourite sound files (Wav only), check **Background audio** and browse to your music file to include it.

7. To set other slideshow options:

   ● Check **Pause on start** in the Control box to pause on the first photo to be displayed. Press the space bar to commence with the slideshow.

   ● Check **Repeat** check box to automatically cycle through the slideshow infinitely.

   ● In the Finish box, check **Create slideshow project** if needed. This will create a clickable thumbnail that stores all your current slideshow settings for future use, e.g.

   ● Check **View slideshow** to see your slideshow immediately after the wizard completes

8. Click the **Finish** button to automatically play your slideshow (by default).

The slideshow is displayed in full screen mode with a supporting slideshow control.

Once the slideshow has run for the first time a slideshow project is created and placed in your **Photos** pane along with your photo thumbnails. This project file saves the slideshow name, photo list, photo order and slideshow properties so that the slideshow can be recalled and edited if necessary. The slideshow project icon is easily spotted—it is made up of a composite of the photos used in your slideshow (see above).

> Hover over the 🖾 icon to view your slideshow's name, photo file names/locations, and the number of photos.

Search You can search for slideshow projects by performing either a Text search (for file name) or a Media Type search (both available from the **Search** button). (See p. 68 and 66).

To delete your photos:

If you change your mind about the photos currently in your slideshow you can select your thumbnail(s) in the main Slideshow window and press the Delete key at any time.

View your slideshow

While your slideshow is running you can use the displayed progress bar to control playback.

● Press the **Pause**, **Stop** or **Next slide** buttons in your slideshow control. The **Play** and **Previous slide** buttons are available after a pause or stop. A progress bar also shows you at what stage your movie is at.

Alternatively, press the space bar to start/stop your slideshow.

> Annoyed by that progress bar? Switch it on or off with the Tab key!

Press the **Esc** key on your keyboard to exit the slideshow at any time.

Edit your slideshow

It's quite likely that you'll want to alter the photo content within your slideshow. New photos may need to be included or existing ones swapped out for alternative photos.

To edit a slideshow:

1.   Locate the slideshow (use the search methods described above).

2.   Double-click the slideshow thumbnail.

3.   From the same Slideshow wizard used to create the slideshow originally, modify settings accordingly.

4.   Click the **Finish** button to save the new slideshow settings.

To add more photos:

Click ⬚Add Photos to add more of your album's photos to the slideshow.

A separate Select Slideshow Photo(s) dialog will display photos within your album but currently absent from your slideshow. Each thumbnail has a check box at its top-right corner—simply check once to have that photo included in the slideshow.

Select any other photos for inclusion then click the ⬚Add Photos button to continue with the slideshow wizard.

Creating a slideshow movie

Once you've created your slideshow and it's saved as a project, you can output your slideshow as a movie (optimized for viewing on your computer monitor). This means your slideshow can be shared across the Internet and be viewable by a wide range of media players.

To create a slideshow movie:

1. Select an existing slideshow project (with ▦ icon), from your **Photos** pane.

2. Click [Create & Share] and then click [▦] **Slideshow Movie**.

3. From the dialog's **Save as type** drop-down menu, select a movie type (*.mpg or *.wmv) to export to.

4. Navigate to a folder to which you'd like to export the movie.

5. Enter a file name for your chosen movie in the **File name** box.

6. Click the **Save** button to save your movie. The resulting pop-up dialog lets you specify the dimensions of your movie. Once set, click the **OK** button.

> ⚲ Now you've created your slideshow, why not upload it to YouTube?

Creating a slideshow VCD

AlbumPlus can export your slideshows as VCD projects, producing a VCD which will play in virtually all DVD players and will also be similarly supported by DVD/CD drives in computers with DVD-playback software. The export process also lets you create your own menus based on one of an impressive array of templates—all easily modified to suit your taste.

VCD writing requirements

● Computer with a DVD-R, DVD-RW, CD-R or CD-RW drive

● CD-R or CD-RW media (normally 700 Mb)

VCD viewing requirements

● For DVD via a TV, a remote control with numeric keypad.

● For computers, a DVD player such as PowerDVD.

Step-by-step

The creation of a slideshow video CD (VCD) is a three-step process—1. Create slideshows, 2. Choose a VCD menu containing the slideshows, then 3. Write the slideshow project to CD. For step 2, selected slideshows can be loaded into a Menu Designer which offers a powerful VCD menu design environment packed full of gallery-driven template presets ready for adoption/editing. You can write slideshows and your chosen VCD menu as a project to CD as the final step.

The slideshow VCD project and all settings are saved in your Album as a Slideshow VCD project, with a unique thumbnail icon.

Simply double-click the thumbnail at any time to reload the project again.

To create your slideshow VCD:

1. Select a slideshow project thumbnail created as described in Creating Slideshows (see p. 85).

2. Click [Create & Share] on the main toolbar, then click **Slideshow VCD**.

3. The **Menu Designer** is launched. This lets you design your own menu based on a selection of pre-designed designs, rearrange slideshow order, change a slideshow's preview photo, and write the project to VCD. Pick a gallery style, background, layout, title style, or thumbnail style, amongst others. For more information, see Menu Designer in AlbumPlus online Help.

4. Click the Menu Designer's **Burn** button.

    The **Write Disc** dialog is used for the disc creation process. Apart from defining your write Speed and device Drive, all you have to do is name your **Disc Label** and click the **Write** button to start the process. Your completed VCD will be ejected once the process is completed.

Navigating your VCD menu

VCD slideshow labels are prefixed with a number when you see the VCD menu on-screen (you won't see the numbers in Menu Designer). Use the numbers on your remote control to pick a chapter. For example, a "4 Per Page" layout will have each thumbnail prefixed with "1. ", "2. ", "3. " and "4. ". Select a number from 1 to 4 to jump to that chapter. If you are on the first page of a multi-page menu, to navigate to the next page, pick the next available number on the remote control (this would be 5 using the example). If you are on the last page of a multi-page menu, to navigate to the previous page, pick the next available number on the remote control (this would again be 5). For any pages in-between, select "5" to jump to a previous page, or select "6" to jump to the next page.

Uploading to YouTube

You may have been aware of the mass popularity of video hosting sites, notably YouTube, in recent years. Placing a movie on YouTube means that you can share a short movie worldwide without writing to media or uploading to your own web site. AlbumPlus can take all of the hard work out of uploading your movies, and can even create and upload your slideshow creations!

> A working YouTube login is required to upload your movies and slideshows. If you don't have a login, visit www.youtube.com and register!

To upload a slideshow or movie file:

1. Select a ⬛ slideshow project thumbnail or a 🎬 movie thumbnail.

2. Click [Create & Share] on the main toolbar, then click **Tube** **Upload to YouTube**.

3. (Optional) In the **Slideshow Movie** dialog, select a **Width** and **Height** for your exported video (it defaults to 480x360). Click **OK**.

4. In the **YouTube Details** dialog:

- Type a title for your movie.

- Select a category from the drop-down list.

- (Optional) Type any additional text in the **Description** text box.

- (Optional) Add tags to your video to help people find your video.

- Click **OK**.

5. In the **YouTube Login** dialog:

- Type in your **Username** and **Password**.

- Check the **Remember password** option to save your login details for future uploads.

- Click **Login**.

6. The progress bar indicates the status of the export and upload processes. Once the upload is complete, it closes automatically.

7. Once the upload is complete, an information dialog will appear to confirm that the movie has been successfully uploaded. Click **OK** to exit.

> Once uploaded, YouTube will process the file. It may take several hours to appear on your YouTube page.

Creating Flash™ slideshows

In AlbumPlus you can create a Flash™ slideshow, using the power of Flash to adopt some eye-catching gallery styles, each offering different ways of cycling through photos. You can create Flash slideshows which let you navigate via a top or bottom control bar or, depending on gallery style, by using:

● thumbnail rollovers (scrollable; with/without reflections)

● vertical thumbnails (scrollable; with/without slide-ins)

● photo grid (scrollable; with slide-ins)

● photo stack (below)

To create a Flash slideshow:

1. Select one or more thumbnails. Use **Shift**-click or **Ctrl**-click to select adjacent or non-adjacent items, respectively.

2. Click ⌐ Create & Share ⌐ and then click ⌐ **Flash Slideshow**.

3.   In the first dialog (Items window):

●   Drag and drop one or more photos to rearrange photo order.

●   Click [Add Photos] to add more photos to your slideshow.

●   Click [View Slideshow] to jump straight to your slideshow.

♀   You can also use your mouse wheel to scroll the window.

4.   Click the **Next>** button.

5.   In the second dialog:

Select a Gallery style from the **Gallery Style** pane running across the top of the displayed dialog. Each type offers a different style for photo navigation—try each one out until you find one you like in the accompanying Preview window. The Preview window displays a small Flash slideshow, which means that you can click on the thumbnails to test each style.

You'll notice a control bar on each style which allows for user navigation of photos after creation.

The last three options only show if background music is used.

6. (Optional) For the selected style, use the **Settings** pane to modify various gallery-wide options (accompanying background music, AutoPlay, etc.). Some options are specific to a gallery style such as enabling/disabling thumbnail rollovers, number of thumbnails shown, photos per stack, etc. Blur amount controls how much blurring occurs between photos. AutoPlay will automatically start photo display at a set but configurable time interval (in seconds). Otherwise, the control bar shown on the Flash slideshow itself can initiate photo playback.

7. (Optional) Click Add Photos to add more photos.

8. Click View Slideshow to view the Flash slideshow in full screen mode. (press **Esc** to exit the full screen view).

9. If you want to save your Flash slideshow, ensure that the **Create Slideshow Project** is checked. Click the **Finish** button.

The Flash slideshow project and all settings are saved in your album as a Flash slideshow project, with a unique thumbnail icon. This project file saves the slideshow name, photo list, photo order and slideshow properties so that it can be recalled and edited if necessary.

Simply double-click the thumbnail at any time to reload the project again.

Ⓠ Hover over the ⓕ icon to view your Flash slideshow's name, photo file names/locations, and the number of photos.

Viewing your Flash slideshow

Your Flash slideshow can be viewed at any time:

1.   Select a Flash slideshow thumbnail.

2.   Click and then click **View Flash Slideshow**.

3.   Use the control bar to navigate your photos.

4.   To exit, press **Esc**.

Editing the Flash slideshow

Once a Flash slideshow project has been created, images can be added or removed. You can also swap your existing gallery style for another, change background music, and set your gallery to autoplay (photos will automatically cycle).

To edit a Flash slideshow:

1.   Select a Flash slideshow thumbnail.

2.   Click and then click **Edit Flash Slideshow**.
     OR

     Double-click the thumbnail.

3.   The Flash Slideshow dialog is displayed. The options available are the same as those available when the slideshow was created.

4.   If you want to save your changes, in the Settings pane, ensure that the **Update slideshow project** option is checked. Click the **Finish** button to save the new slideshow settings.

To add more photos:

From within the Flash Slideshow dialog, click ⬚Add Photos⬚ to add more of your album's photos to the slideshow.

A separate Select Slideshow Photo(s) dialog will display photos within your album but currently absent from your slideshow. Each thumbnail has a check box at its top-right corner—simply check once to have that photo included in the slideshow.

Select any other photos for inclusion then click the [Add Photos] button to continue with the Flash slideshow wizard.

To delete your photos:

If you change your mind about the photos currently in your slideshow, edit the project and from the first Flash Slideshow dialog, select the thumbnail(s) that you want to remove and press the **Delete** key.

Publishing your Flash slideshow

In AlbumPlus you can publish your Flash slideshow and turn it into files that can be displayed on a web page. The published page is exported as "index.html" and has two associated folders, "apimages" and "apscripts". These contain the files needed to display the Flash slideshow in an Internet browser.

To publish a Flash slideshow:

1. Select a Flash slideshow thumbnail.

2. Click 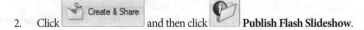 and then click **Publish Flash Slideshow**.

3. In the **Browse For Folder** dialog, choose a destination for the exported files. Click **OK**.

4. The slideshow will open in your default browser.

Sharing by mobile device

AlbumPlus allows you to send any photo or media file directly to any Internet-enabled device (typically a mobile phone, BlackBerry, PDA, etc.) at reduced image dimensions to fit your phone's physical screen dimensions. The only pre-requisite is that you'll need to know the recipients email address in advance. You may also know the screen dimensions of the recipient's device in advance of sending, so you can set the optimum image size.

Several factors external to AlbumPlus will govern whether the photos can be viewed by the email recipient. These include whether:

- the device supports Internet connectivity.

- the device has an operational email address (and can receive attachments).

- the recipient's network supports email attachments.

- a suitable service agreement is in place.

- for emails sent internationally, sender and recipient's carriers have international roaming agreements.

To send to mobile:

1.   Select one or more thumbnails. Use **Shift**-click or **Ctrl**-click to select adjacent or non-adjacent items, respectively.

2.   Click [Create & Share] on the main toolbar, then click [ ] **Send to Mobile**.

3.   From the dialog:

- To retain original photo sizes, enable **Keep original dimensions**.
       OR

- To reduce your photo to a set pixel width, enable the **Small** or **Large** option (this compresses the file, reducing file size). The former option is recommended for mobile phones. (The biggest pixel dimension of the original photo will be reduced to a 96 or 120 pixel width).
  OR

- Enable **Limit image dimensions to a maximum of** and select a suitable image resolution—this will be the new pixel height or width.

4. Click **OK**.

5. From your currently open or launched email program, an email message is created with your photos attached. Click the **Send** button when you've filled in the destination email address (**To**), **Subject** line, and message.

Sharing photos by email

The widespread availability of the Internet means that most people's family and friends are now only a quick email away. Higher line speeds via ISDN and now Broadband connections also open up new opportunities for sharing not just one or two photos but whole photo collections easily.

AlbumPlus directs selected photos from within its user interface to either a Standard or web-based email program, for subsequent mailing.

To email photo(s):

1. Select one or more thumbnails. Use **Shift**-click or **Ctrl**-click to select adjacent or non-adjacent items, respectively.

2. Click on the main toolbar, then click **Send to email**.

3. From the dialog:

   - To minimize file size, set a limiting image size—enter a pixel height/width into the input box.

- To change file type to JPG (this compresses the file, reducing file size), enable the **Convert to JPEG** option.

- Enable Standard or Browser-based email output options.

4. From your currently open or launched email program, an email message is created with your photos attached. Click the **Send** button when your email is completed.

Setting your Image Size

AlbumPlus allows you to send any photo directly by email with an added file size limiter if necessary. This avoids sending large file sizes—this could affect your popularity, especially for recipients with dial-up modems!

Click the **Limit image dimensions to a maximum of** radio button and select a suitable image resolution—this will be the new pixel height or width (the biggest pixel dimension of the original photo will be reduced to the new image size). Alternatively, keep the file's original image dimensions.

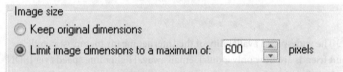

Image size
◯ Keep original dimensions
◉ Limit image dimensions to a maximum of: 600 pixels

Setting the File type

To take advantage of better file compression (i.e., smaller file sizes) you may want to convert your image to JPEG if not already in this format. The compression used is 100%, which retains photo quality. The conversion would be suitable for uncompressed photo formats (i.e., those of a large file size) such as RAW and TIF.

To select, click the **Convert to JPEG** radio button. Alternatively, keep the file's original format.

File type
◯ Keep original
◉ Convert to JPEG

Choosing standard or browser-based email

The two options reflect your personal email preference. Some users use an email account set up through their own Internet Service Provider (ISP). Others, especially when travelling, prefer the flexibility of a browser-based email solution (e.g., www.yahoo.com, www.hotmail.com, etc.).

● **Standard** email: Enable the **Attach to new email message** radio button. This will launch an untitled email dialog with the photos already attached.

● **Browser-based** email. Enable the **Save to folder** radio button and specify a destination folder by entering a new file location or browsing to it via the ▦ button. The option will copy all your selected photos to a single chosen location—these photos can then be uploaded to your browser-based email session.

Output

○ Attach to new email message (Standard email)

◉ Save to folder (Browser-based email)

Destination folder

C:\Users\cwilson\Documents   [...]

🔋 An Internet connection is required for the emailing of pictures.

Creating screensavers

If you like to customize the look and feel of your PC's desktop, it's likely that you've applied a Windows-supplied screensaver (or your own) in the past. If you haven't done this before, a screensaver is a temporary mode which will display a set of photos when your PC has been inactive after a set time period; the screensaver mode is exited when you reuse your keyboard or mouse again.

> The term "screensaver" is historical; they were used in an earlier
> computing era to prevent a fixed image from being burned into the
> phosphor of the less sophisticated monitor screens of the time. The
> function is now reserved for entertainment or security purposes
> only.

From AlbumPlus's perspective, you can create a slideshow or flying screensaver
"project" from selected photos, then activate the **Serif AlbumPlus** screensaver
from the Windows desktop (as you would to activate all other screensavers).

To create your screensaver:

1. Select one or more thumbnails. Use **Shift**-click or **Ctrl**-click to select
   adjacent or non-adjacent items, respectively.

2. Click 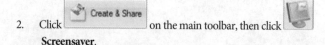 on the main toolbar, then click
   Screensaver.

3. From the dialog, choose a type of slideshow:

- **Slideshow**: Enable the option to create a traditional slide-by-slide presentation with fading between each photo. Optionally, modify the time that each slide is displayed on-screen (Slide duration) and/or the time for each fade (Fade duration).

   OR

- **Flying**: Enable the option to display photos, as thumbnails, which move around your screen. Optionally, set the speed of movement (**Speed** slider) and/or number of image shown (**Images**).

4. Click **OK**.

Once created, the screensaver is automatically activated. You can change the settings from the Windows desktop or via Control Panel.

Setting your PC wallpaper

You may be familiar with changing the wallpaper in Windows by right-clicking on the desktop, and changing the background from **Properties>Desktop**.

From within AlbumPlus, you can make any selected photo in your album become your Windows wallpaper with equally minimal effort. The feature works on a single photo and, subject to a check for how you want to present the photo, will show your photo in the Windows background.

To set new wallpaper:

1. Select a thumbnail for your chosen photo.

2. Click on the main toolbar, then click
   Wallpaper.

3. From the dialog, choose:

- **Actual Size**: The photo is centred on the screen and its original dimensions are preserved.
  OR

- **Tiled**: Multiple copies of the photo are tiled together on the screen.
  OR

- **Stretched**: The chosen photo is stretched to fit screen dimensions.

4. Click **OK**. Your wallpaper appears on your desktop.

Creating panoramas

 If you have Serif PanoramaPlus (version 3 or later) installed, you can create seamless panoramas from your photos.

To create a panorama:

1. In the Photos pane, select the photos that you want to 'stitch' together.

20/04/2004   20/04/2004   20/04/2004   20/04/2004

20/04/2004   20/04/2004   20/04/2004   20/04/2004

2. Click **Create & Share**, then click **Panorama**.

3. PanoramaPlus opens and your photos are automatically stitched together as a panorama. Export the panorama as an image (**File>Export as image...**) and close PanoramaPlus. (For more information, see the PanoramaPlus Help.)

4. Your new image will appear in the AlbumPlus Get photo(s) dialog. Click **Get Photos**.

5. Your new panorama appears in the Photos pane.

Creating calendars

Not to be confused with AlbumPlus's Year View and Month View modes (which offer interactive "live" calendars"), AlbumPlus's creative calendars offer beautiful print-ready calendar designs. Just like all Create & Share activities, you can populate a calendar with chosen photos and give it that personalized "look and feel". If you've used the diary or events feature in Year View or Month View mode, they'll also appear in your calendar.

> The design method is identical to that used for creating postcards, greetings cards, and photo albums.

AlbumPlus can save each calendar design as a project (with all settings stored) which can be retrieved at a later date. Look for a Calendar Project thumbnail (example opposite), from which the project can be loaded again by double-clicking.

To create a calendar:

1. Select one or more photo thumbnails for your album. Use **Shift**-click or **Ctrl**-click to select adjacent or non-adjacent items, respectively.

2. Click ![Create & Share], then click ![icon] **Calendars**.

3. From the dialog, set a calendar **Start Month** (defaults to current month) and an **End Month**. You can create a yearly calendar by setting, e.g. Jan 2009 to Dec 2009, respectively. Click the **OK** button.

4. From the Calendar Theme dialog, click on a theme category of your choice from the left-most vertical pane and then pick a thumbnail from the right menu pane (this theme will be applied throughout your calendar). Click **OK**.

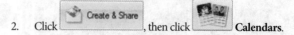

WARNING: Selecting a different theme subsequently will revert your entire project, losing all your design settings.

5. In the launched design studio, review each page layout (there will be twelve to reflect each month of the year). You have the option to swap any layout from single- to dual-photo, or use a layout with rotated picture frame(s).

6. Select any unwanted page layout from the left pane, and click the **Designs** button on the toolbar. Pick an alternative layout from the Designs pane. Repeat for each layout until you have a preferred page layout for each month.

7. To swap a selected page's background, click the **Backgrounds** button and, from the flyout menu, choose a new background thumbnail. Repeat for each layout. Your page design is complete!

8. Drag your photos from the lower pane onto photo placeholders (indicated by "Drag your photo here" text), then fine-tune the photo positioning if needed.

   Optionally, use the **Add Photos** button at the bottom of the screen to populate the photo's pane with more photos if needed.

9. To save your design, select the **Save and Close** button on the top toolbar.
   OR

   Click the **Close** button. (You'll be asked if you want to save as a project).

To adjust your photo's positioning:

● Hover over your placed photo to display a photo bar hosting a range of one-click adjustment tools.

Use any of the tools to zoom or position your photo to you liking; the Reset button reverts the photo back to its original zoom level and position.

Creating photo albums

AlbumPlus allows you to make more creative use of your photos. Especially popular with photos is the electronic equivalent of the traditional photo album, where you benefit from being able to swap in and out photos, pick supporting designs, and output to your printer quickly and simply.

The creation of your photo album is very straight forward, and centres around four main creative steps.

- **Photo selection**—choose special photos for your album.

- **Themes**—select from themes such as kids, occasions, abstract, or more simplistic themes.

- **Designs**—select a photos-per-page layout.

- **Backgrounds**—choose a background to complement your photos.

You'll start with a set number of pages (shown vertically) each adopting a different layout design. Once you've picked a theme, it's unlikely that you'll want to keep the different displayed layouts, preferring to swap any unwanted page layouts with more preferable ones from the **Designs** button (top toolbar), e.g. you may want to concentrate on two-photos-per-page layouts throughout. Once your design layout is decided, you can increase/decrease the number of pages to match the number of chosen photos.

> The design method is identical to that used for creating calendars, greetings cards, and postcards.

AlbumPlus can save each photo album design as a project (with all settings stored) which can be retrieved at a later date. Look for a Photo Album Project thumbnail (example opposite), from which the project can be loaded and edited again by double-clicking.

To create a photo album:

1. Select one or more photo thumbnails for your album. Use **Shift**-click or **Ctrl**-click to select adjacent or non-adjacent items, respectively.

2. Click on the main toolbar, then click [ ] **Photo Album** button.

3. From the Photo Album Theme dialog, click on a theme category of your choice from the left-most vertical pane and then pick a thumbnail from the displayed menu pane (this theme will be applied throughout your album). Click **OK**.

    ❗ WARNING: Selecting a different theme will revert your entire project, losing all your design settings.

4. In the design studio, select any unwanted page layouts from the left pane, replacing it with a layout from the Designs pane (click the **Designs** button). Pick a layout category based on the required number of photos per page (e.g., 1 per page, 2 per page, etc.), then a specific layout. Repeat for each layout until you have your ideal set of page layouts. Alternatively, duplicate a selected layout by clicking the **Add Page** button (the duplicate will appear immediately after the selected layout). Use the **Delete Page** button to remove any selected page.

5. To swap a selected page's background, click the **Backgrounds** button and, from the flyout menu, choose a new background thumbnail. Your album design is complete!

6. Select each page in turn and drag photos from the lower pane onto each photo placeholder (indicated by "Drag your photo here" text), then fine-tune each photo's position if needed.

    Optionally, use the [ ] **Add Photos** button at the bottom of the screen to populate the photo's pane with more photos if needed.

7. (Optional) Click [ ] **Print** from the top toolbar to output your photo album to your printer.

    ❓ For Landscape printing, remember to adjust page orientation via your printer's Properties.

8.   To save your photo album, click **Save and Close** on the top toolbar.
      OR

      Click the **Close** button. (You'll be asked if you want to save as a project).

Creating greetings cards

 Single-page single-photo greetings cards are simple and fun to
produce in AlbumPlus. With the minimum of design effort you can create your
own folded Greetings Card, meaning no more expensive trips to the card shop!

Simply choose a Theme, Design and Background on which to base your
Greetings Card. The design method is similar to that used for creating calendars,
postcards, and photo albums.

AlbumPlus saves each Greetings Card
design as a project (with all settings
stored) which can be loaded and edited at
a later date by double-clicking. Look for a
Greetings Card Project thumbnail
(example opposite).

To create a Greetings Card:

1.   Select a photo to be used in your greetings card.

2.   Click [Create & Share] on the main toolbar, then click
      Greetings Card.

3.   From the Greeting Card Theme dialog, click on a theme category of your
      choice from the left-most vertical pane and then pick a thumbnail from the
      displayed menu pane (this theme will be applied throughout your design).
      Click **OK**.

> ⬤ WARNING: Selecting a different theme subsequent to this will revert your entire project, losing all your design settings.

4. (Optional) In the design studio, select a different design from the Designs pane (click **Designs** button).

5. To swap a selected page's background, click the **Backgrounds** button and, from the flyout menu, choose a new background thumbnail. Your page design is complete!

6. Drag your photo from the lower pane onto the photo placeholder (indicated by "Drag your Photo here" text), then fine-tune the photo's positioning if needed.

   Optionally, use the **Add Photos** button at the bottom of the screen to introduce a replacement photo which can be swapped for the current photo by drag and drop.

7. Don't forget to add your card Title. Click on the title text and type your own title message.

8. (Optional) Click **Print** from the top toolbar to output your design to your printer.

> ⬤ Remember to set the printer to Landscape—this lets you print and then fold your paper to create a stunning Greetings Card.

9. To save your Greetings Card, click **Save and Close** button on the top toolbar.
   OR

   Click the **Close** button. (You'll be asked if you want to save as a project).

Creating postcards

Postcards rival greetings cards as the simplest projects that you can create in AlbumPlus. Their creation uses a similar procedure to that used for creating calendars, greetings cards, and photo albums. Like Greetings Card projects they are single-page projects, but differ in that they support multiple photos on the page and are output to A6 print size (14.8cm x 10.5cm) instead of A5 print size (21cm X 14.8cm) for greetings cards.

If you're printing to A4 paper you'll have to cut your postcard out from the A4 printout.

AlbumPlus can save each postcard design as a project (with all settings stored) which can be loaded and edited at a later date by double-clicking. Look for a Postcard Project thumbnail (example opposite).

To create a postcard:

1. Select a photo to be used in your postcard.

2. Click **Create & Share** on the main toolbar, then click **Postcard**.

3. From the Postcard Theme dialog, click on a theme category of your choice from the left-most vertical pane and then pick a thumbnail from the displayed menu pane (this theme will be applied throughout your design). Click **OK**.

> 🔋 WARNING: Selecting a different theme subsequent to this will revert your entire project, losing all your design settings.

4. Optional) In the design studio, select a different design from the Designs pane (click **Designs** button). Pick a design category based on the required number of photos per page (e.g., 1 per page, 2 per page, etc.), then a specific layout.

5. To swap a selected page's background, click the **Backgrounds** button and, from the flyout menu, choose a new background thumbnail. Your page design is complete!

6. Drag your photos from the lower pane onto photo placeholders (indicated by "Drag your photo here" text), then fine-tune the photo positioning if needed.

    Optionally, use the **Add Photos** button at the bottom of the screen to populate the photo's pane with more photos if needed.

7. Don't forget to add your card Title. Click on the title text and type your own title message.

8. (Optional) Click the **Print** button from the top toolbar to output your design to your printer.

9. To save your design, select the **Save and Close** button on the top toolbar.
    OR

    Click the **Close** button. (You'll be asked if you want to save as a project).

Uploading to Facebook

Facebook is a social networking website that enables you to keep in touch with friends, and amongst other things, upload an unlimited number of photos. In AlbumPlus, your photos can be shared with friends and family in just a few clicks!

> A working Facebook login is required to upload your photos. If you don't have a login, visit www.facebook.com and register!

To upload photos to Facebook:

1. Select the photo thumbnails that you want to upload.

2. Click on the main toolbar, then click **fb** **Upload to Facebook**.

3. In the Facebook login dialog, type in your email address and password and click **Login**.

Facebook Login

AlbumPlus

Login to Facebook to enjoy the full functionality of AlbumPlus. If you don't want this to happen, go to the normal Facebook login page.

Email: test@hotmail.com

Password: •••••••••

Optional: ☑ Save my login info to avoid logging in to Facebook again to use this application.

Login or Sign up for Facebook

Forgot your password?

> 🚨 If this is the first time you have uploaded to Facebook with AlbumPlus, you'll need to authorize AlbumPlus to access your account. When prompted, click the Allow button.

4. When prompted, click **OK** to close the dialog and start the photo upload.

Uploading photo 1 of 12

The progress bar indicates the status of the export and upload processes. Once the upload is complete, it closes automatically.

Once your photos have been uploaded, your default web browser opens. You may need to verify your Facebook username and password. In the **Pending photos page** you will need to 'approve' the uploaded photos. Select the images and click **Approve Selected Photos** to complete the upload process.

5. Close the browser window to return to AlbumPlus.

Uploading to flickr

Flickr is an online photo and video management website. It is a great place to share your photos with people all over the world. AlbumPlus makes it easy to upload your favourite photos.

> A working Flickr account is required to upload your photos. This is your Yahoo! ID. If you don't have a login ID or account, you can create one the first time you upload your photos. Alternatively, register at www.flickr.com.

To upload photos to Flickr:

1. Select the photo thumbnails that you want to upload.

2. Click **Create & Share** on the main toolbar, then click **r** **Upload to Flickr**.

3. In the Flickr upload dialog, you can set the image size. AlbumPlus will resample your photos accordingly, while retaining the aspect ratio.

4. Click **OK**. The Flickr login dialog opens. If necessary, type in your Yahoo! ID and Password and click **Sign In**.

> If this is the first time you have uploaded to Flickr with AlbumPlus, you will need to authorize AlbumPlus to access your account. When prompted, click the Ok, I'll allow it button. If you've also just created a new Flickr account, choose your Flickr screen name and click Create a New Account.

5.   When prompted, click **OK** to close the Flickr Login dialog and start the photo upload.

Uploading photo 1 of 12

The progress bar indicates the status of the export and upload processes. Once the upload is complete, it closes automatically.

Once your photos have been uploaded, your default web browser opens. You may need to verify your Flickr account password. In the Your new additions page, you can give your photos titles, tags and a description. Click **OK** to update the information. Close the browser window to return to AlbumPlus.

Manipulating
Photos

6

Manipulating photos

Fix & Enhance It is highly likely that at some time or another the photos you spent valuable time taking have not turned out as well as you had expected. Don't worry—AlbumPlus supports several photo editing operations from the main toolbar's **Fix & Enhance** button that can radically improve your end results.

Here's a quick summary of each option.

 Opens QuickFix Studio. Here you can make various adjustments to your image—crop, straighten, Auto Fix, darken/lighten, brightness/contrast, colour cast, colour saturation, sharpen and fix red eye.

 Opens Instant Artist Studio. Here you can apply various artistic effects to your photos.

 Opens Makeover Studio. Here you can give the subject of your photo a complete makeover—whiten teeth, apply fake tan, remove dark circles, brighten eyes, remove blemishes and smooth skin.

 Opens the image in PhotoPlus for advanced photo editing.

 Rotates the image anti-clockwise in 90° intervals.

 Rotates the image clockwise in 90° intervals.

 Flips the image horizontally.

Flips the image vertically.

    Opens the Revert Manager dialog where you can choose to "undo" changes and revert to an earlier version of the image. (For more information, see **Revert Manager** in online Help.)

> Attempts to correct photos may not always give you perfect results first time. As a general rule try the above methods to experiment until you get the desired effect. Remember that you can always undo your work or revert photos.

Navigating in the studios

All of the studios—QuickFix, Makeover and Instant Artist—have a similar interface.

Available adjustments are found on the toolbar at the top of the studio. To apply, click on the adjustment name then alter its adjustment options in the left pane. Depending on the type of adjustment, a selection of sliders, check boxes, and drop-down menus can be modified (you can also enter absolute values into available input boxes). Whatever settings are changed, the image preview will be adjusted automatically to reflect the new settings.

A series of display buttons under your preview window let you preview your photo in different ways.

From left to right, you can display in a single window, or either as portrait/landscape dual-screen or vertical/horizontal split-screen for before and after views.

For further control of your display, use the lower-right Navigator thumbnail to **Zoom to Fit**, view **Actual Size**, or incrementally zoom via buttons or slider. By default, you'll be able to pan around your zoomed-in image with the hand cursor at any time.

To exit the studio:

● Click **Save** to exit and save your changes to the original image.

● Click **Save As** to exit and save your changes as a separate image.

● Click **Cancel** to exit without saving.

Using QuickFix Studio

QuickFix Studio, a powerful photo correction solution, can be used to perform image correction within AlbumPlus.

To launch QuickFix Studio:

1. Select a photo for adjustment.

2. Click **Fix & Enhance** on the main toolbar.

3. Click **QuickFix Studio**.

The QuickFix Studio user interface typically consists of a main photo preview window, a Tools toolbar and a tool-specific Image Adjustment pane.

Tools toolbar

How To pane

Image Adjustment Pane

Navigation thumbnail

Zoom controls

Preview display controls

Undo/ Redo

The Image Adjustment Pane will change depending on which function is selected, i.e. the tools for adjusting brightness will differ from those for fixing red eye.

Here is a quick summary of how you would use each tool. You'll find each explained in more detail (with supporting examples) in AlbumPlus help and for Step-by-Step instructions, see the Studio's How To pane.

Tool Name	Use it to..
Crop Tool	Retain a specific area of a photo while discarding the remainder.
Straighten Tool	Correct a crooked image.
Auto Fix	Apply an automatic contrast adjustment.
Brightness/Contrast	Adjust lightness/darkness and tonal range.

Darken/Lighten	Adjust highlights and shadows.
Colour Cast	Adjust colour irregularities.
Colour Saturation	Adjust colour intensity.
Sharpen	Make your photo look crisper in appearance.
Red Eye	Correct the "red eye" phenomenon common in colour photos.

Using Instant Artist Studio

Instant Artist Studio will bring your artistic side out—creating your own masterpieces by picking from a variety of classic painting styles (with no paint splashes!). The tool will transform your image in a single-click. Classic styles include Expressionist, Impressionist, Oil, and many others. More abstract styles are available such as Munchist.

Whichever style you choose, you can take advantage of Instant Artist's powerful studio environment. This provides a resizable dialog with large scale preview window, a thumbnail gallery showing each effect (for visual clues), and a comprehensive range of context-sensitive effect settings. Instant Artist's interruptible redraw also means that you can make changes to your settings without waiting for your image to refresh; the effect will be redrawn immediately.

To launch Instant Artist Studio:

1. Select a photo for adjustment.

2. Click **Fix & Enhance** on the main toolbar.

3.   Click **Instant Artist Studio**. The Instant Artist Studio
     environment is displayed.

4.   Select an effect's thumbnail from the thumbnail pane. You'll see your
     image update to reflect the new effect.

5.   To see a different part of the image, drag it with the hand cursor. Click
     the Zoom buttons to zoom in or out.

6.   Adjust the sliders (or enter specific values) to vary the effect. If
     necessary, click the Default button to revert to the standard settings for
     this effect.

7.   Click **OK** to apply the effect, or Cancel to abandon changes.

The Instant Artist Studio user interface typically consists of a main photo
preview window, a Tools toolbar and a tool-specific Image Adjustment pane.

Tools toolbar

How To
pane

Image
Adjustment
Pane

Navigation
thumbnail

Zoom
controls

Preview
display controls

Undo/
Redo

The Image Adjustment Pane will change depending on which function is selected, i.e. the tools for stained glass effect will differ from those for oil painting effect.

> The effects shown in the preview pane are not fully rendered as this would take too much time to see the effect. This means that they will appear slightly different at different zoom levels. To see the true effect save the changes to file!

Here is a quick summary of how you would use each tool. You'll find each explained in more detail (with supporting examples) in AlbumPlus help and for Step-by-Step instructions, see the Studio's How To pane.

Tool Name	Use it to..
Stained Glass	Divide the image into irregular fragments similar to a stained glass or mosaic.
Comic Book	Posterize the image edges to produce an effect commonly encountered in classic action-hero comics.
Black & White	Convert your image into black & white, adjust the colour saturation or give it sepia tones.
Expressionist	Add "brush strokes" including random colour offsets of variable brush size.
Munchist	Broadens and enhances colour regions into streaks.
Impressionist	Broadens and enhances colour regions into blotches.
Oil	Adds bristled "brush strokes" with variable size, plus various settings to preserve the degree of detail retained from the original image.
Pencil	Renders the image using greyscale strokes of variable size.

| Pointillist | "Dabs on" small dots (instead of painting with linear strokes as in the Oil effect), of variable size. |
| Water Colour | Simulates relatively desaturated colours on a textured canvas, with control over the amount of image detail preserved. |

Using Makeover Studio

Makeover Studio, delivers professional retouching techniques such as whitening of teeth and eyes, smoothing skin, and reducing under-the-eye shadows within AlbumPlus.

To launch Makeover Studio:

1.   Select a photo for adjustment.

2.   Click **Fix & Enhance** on the main toolbar.

3.   Click **Makeover Studio**.

The Makeover Studio user interface typically consists of a main photo preview window, a Tools toolbar and a tool-specific Image Adjustment pane.

Tools toolbar

How To pane

Image Adjustment Pane

Navigation thumbnail

Zoom controls

Preview display controls

Undo/ Redo

The Image Adjustment Pane will change depending on which function is selected, i.e. the tools for whitening teeth will differ from those for smoothing skin.

Here is a quick summary of how you would use each tool. You'll find each explained in more detail (with supporting examples) in AlbumPlus help and for Step-by-Step instructions, see the Studio's How To pane.

Tool Name	Use it to..
Whiten Teeth	Brighten the person's smile without the expensive trip to the dentist!
Fake Tan	Add a realistic summer glow to the skin.
Remove Dark Circles	Replace dark under-eye shadows.
Brighten Eyes	Brighten the whites of the eyes.

| Remove Blemishes | Quickly remove blemishes with a single click. |
| Smooth Skin | Soften wrinkles and give skin a smoother appearance. |

Reading a Histogram

Histograms can be used to view the Red (R), Green (G), Blue (B) and composite (RGB) channels for the current photo. The histogram does not allow adjustment of the image but is useful for evaluating colour distribution throughout channels and any photo colour deficiencies at a glance. By assessing this distribution you may then wish to apply an adjustment with the available QuickFix Studio feature, or use Serif PhotoPlus for more advanced image editing options.

To view a photo's histogram:

1. Select an image thumbnail.

2. Click [☰ Display] and then select Photo Information from the drop-down list to open the Photo Information dialog.

3. Click [▦] at the top of the dialog. Under the Properties box, showing image size, resolution, and bit depth, the initial histogram is displayed for All channels (composite).

4. (Optional) Pick an individual channel from the **Channels** drop-down box to isolate a Red, Green, or Blue channel.

5. If necessary, adjust the photo with an appropriate editing tool.

Understanding the histogram

At first sight, the histogram of any photo appears a little daunting. Let's look at a typical histogram.

The histogram, when Channels is set to "All", shows pixel distribution spread across overlapping red, green, and blue channels. Where an overlap occurs between two or more channels, the resulting colour is given a separate colour. For example, red and blue will show purple.

For simplicity, let's display a red channel (below). The **horizontal X axis** represents the extent of red tones (as shadows, midtones and highlights), expressed as a number between 0 and 255, where 0 represents the number of red pixels of value 0, and 255 represents the number of red pixels of value 255.

The **vertical Y axis** is the relative number of red pixels at each of the 255 values on the X axis, described above. The higher the graph is at any level, the more red pixels reside at that particular level.

Editing photos in Serif PhotoPlus

If you're the proud owner of Serif PhotoPlus (version 10 or later) you may find it invaluable to be able to perform some professional image editing on your album content. From within AlbumPlus itself it's possible to launch PhotoPlus directly.

To launch a photo in Serif PhotoPlus:

1. Select the photo thumbnail in any mode.

2. Either:

    *   Click [Fix & Enhance] on the main toolbar, then click
        Edit in PhotoPlus.
        OR

    *   Right-click the thumbnail, select FixPhoto, and then Edit in PhotoPlus. Serif PhotoPlus will be launched automatically (if installed).

    Make your image adjustment in PhotoPlus, ensuring that you use the **Save Original** option on the **File** menu to save your file. Changes made will be shown in AlbumPlus—your photo thumbnail will update automatically.

Creating your first panorama

7

The following steps will help you to get started with creating panoramas. We'll show you how to import some sample images, stitch them into a panorama, and then export the finished panorama.

Before you begin, we recommend that you take a few minutes to get acquainted with the PanoramaPlus workspace. If you haven't already done so, review the **Understanding the user interface** and **Visual reference** topics in the Online help. Once you've done that, you're ready to import your source images and create your first panorama.

Importing source images

1. Open **PanoramaPlus**.

2. In the Startup Wizard, choose **start from scratch**.

3. On the main toolbar, click the [Add] button, (you can also click **File>Add Photos**, or press **Ctrl + 1**).

4. In the **Add Photos** dialog, browse to your PanoramaPlus installation directory (usually **C:\Program Files\Serif\PanoramaPlus\3.0**).

5. In the **Samples\Loch Lomond** folder, hold down the **Shift** key, and then click to select the three image files (**Lomond_1.jpg** to **Lomond_3.jpg**).

6. Click **Open**.

   The images display in the **Source Images** pane of the PanoramaPlus workspace.

Creating your panorama

In the **Source Images** pane, you can select the images you want to use for your panorama, or you can omit this step and let PanoramaPlus use all the images displayed. You can also rotate, reorder, resize, and delete your source images as required.

1. Click the ![Stitch] button (you can also click **File>Stitch**, or press **Ctrl + 2**).

   The panorama displays in the **Panorama** pane and the **Navigator** pane. In the **Panorama** pane, the title bar displays the current image size and zoom level.

> 🖐 Use the **View** toolbar at the lower left of the workspace to change your viewing options.

   When PanoramaPlus stitches the source images into a panorama, it often results in a panorama with uneven borders. Unless your source images are perfectly aligned, which is unlikely, you'll need to crop your panorama so that its edges are squared off. PanoramaPlus provides several different ways of cropping an image.

2. Click the ![Crop] tool, then in the **Panorama** pane, adjust the red crop outline by clicking and dragging the square crop 'handles.'

   - or -

Click the button, and then select a crop size from the drop-down list. The crop outline adjusts to the selected crop size.

3. When you are happy with your finished panorama, you're ready to export it. (PanoramaPlus will crop your image during the export process.)

    You can export your panorama as a graphic file, as a PDF, or as a QuickTime virtual reality (VR) movie. In the following steps, we'll show you how to export your panorama as a JPEG file.

Exporting your panorama as a JPEG file

1. On the toolbar, click the **Share** button and select **Export Panorama** from the drop-down list (you can also click **File>Export Panorama** or press **Ctrl + 3**).

    In the **Export Panorama** dialog, your panorama displays in the **Preview** pane. The **Size** and **Options** sections provide the settings and file formats that you can apply to your exported image.

Let's resize this image and export it as a JPEG file.

2.   In the **Size** section, click **Resize**.

3.   In the **Resize** dialog, in the **Width** box, type '600.'

4.   Click **OK**.

The panorama is generated and the new dimensions are displayed in the **Export** dialog.

5. In the **Options** section, in the **Format** drop-down list, you can choose to export to other file formats instead of the JPEG graphics format (default).

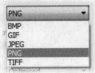

Once you've chosen your settings, the preview image is updated to reflect the changes. At the lower left of the **Options** section, note that the size of the file is also updated.

6. Click **OK**.

7. In the **Save As** dialog, choose the save location and name for your panorama, and then click **Save**.

That's all there is to it! In these few short steps, you've created a panorama and exported it as a JPEG file.

You can also send your panorama as an email attachment, or print it out.

Index

8